Teens Have Style!

Teens Have Style!

Fashion Programs for Young Adults at the Library

Sharon Snow and Yvonne Reed

 LIBRARIES UNLIMITED

AN IMPRINT OF ABC-CLIO, LLC
Santa Barbara, California • Denver, Colorado • Oxford, England

Library of Congress Cataloging-in-Publication Data

Snow, Sharon.
    Teens have style! : fashion programs for young adults at the library / Sharon Snow
and Yvonne Reed.
        pages cm
    Includes bibliographical references and index.
    ISBN 978-1-59884-892-2 (pbk.) — ISBN 978-1-59884-893-9 (ebook)
  1. Young adults' libraries—Activity programs.   2. Libraries and teenagers.   3. Fashion design.
4. Teenagers—Clothing.   I. Reed, Yvonne, 1974–   II. Title.
    Z718.5.S66 2013
    027.62'6—dc23   2012041226

ISBN: 978-1-59884-892-2
EISBN: 978-1-59884-893-9

17 16 15 14 13   1 2 3 4 5

This book is also available on the World Wide Web as an eBook.
Visit www.abc-clio.com for details.

Libraries Unlimited
An Imprint of ABC-CLIO, LLC

ABC-CLIO, LLC
130 Cremona Drive, P.O. Box 1911
Santa Barbara, California 93116-1911

This book is printed on acid-free paper ∞

Manufactured in the United States of America

Contents

Introduction:
It's All about Style

When we first begin to dress ourselves, we begin to develop our own style and opinions on what we should or should not wear. Clothes and style allow both 'tweens and teens to express who they are. As teens find that sense of style, they begin to feel a great sense of self. Clothes and style allow for character and personalities to emerge in a safe and nonthreatening way. It is healthy for teens to be able to express their personalities, and fashion is one of the greatest ways to do so.

If you are going to have successful programs, you must acknowledge the fact that peer pressure is a reason for many in this age group to follow the trends without being ridiculed, and you must build from that foundation. They will need assurance that they can adapt a trend to work for them if they realize that fashion trends come from many sources, such as movies and music. Fashion programming is a way to make the library relevant to their world.

Teens Have Style! is a programming book for librarians, teachers, and recreational leaders who work with young people in sixth through twelfth grades. The emphasis is on the library, though others working with this age group may have other spaces and groups for programming, and they will find these ideas valuable. They may offer ideas for collaboration between agencies.

In recent years libraries have become the gathering place for teens, a place to hang out with friends in a safe and free environment. You and your colleagues can provide information and resources about current styles and trends, making the library an excellent place for 'tweens and teens to gather to talk about fashion. Your programs will allow them to experiment with different looks and styles without investing in expensive clothes.

Recently, there has been some discussion about how librarians can attract more teenage girls into the library. What better way than fashion? To help you with this, we have put together a group of programs to capture 'tweens' and teens' interests in fashion. Although many of these programs will appeal more to young women, there will be many programs that will also appeal to young men. Remember, where the girls are, the boys will follow.

Programming is important to a library. First, it brings in teens who might not be regular library users. Second, it creates partnerships. Many of the programs involve getting community support by asking for speakers, donations of prizes, and judging contests. Some of the ways to create partnerships are the following:

- Get to know your community by collecting business cards from community members that may someday be a resource for library programs.
- Create a file with these business cards and other names you discover.
- Read the local newspaper. This is an excellent way to become familiar with people and resources for future programs. Keep a list of names, contact information, and whatever

talent or career that might be of use in a program. Recently, in the local newspaper there were two articles about women who were in fashion. One helps young women enter beauty pageants. She would be a good resource for teaching teens how to walk in high heels for a prom program. The other woman makes one-of-a-kind shoes. She would be an excellent speaker when doing the "Transform Your Shoes" program.

- Place group contacts and potential contacts into categories, such as food, fashion, art, etc.
- Refer back to your file during the program planning process for ideas of possible presenters for your programs.

Each chapter includes a series of programs with activities, hands-on projects, instructions, photos, and a bibliography. The programs range from very easy to more complex. Many of the programs are economical while others require more funding. All of the ideas can be mixed and matched. If a program is too complex, it is easy to leave out a few activities to fit the time constraints or the spaces available in your library.

Some of the more complex programs are good for creating community partnerships. If you are limited in space in your library or if the program would be better presented at another venue, you will have opportunities to work with your community partners.

All the books in the bibliography have current material published within the past six years, with a few exceptions. Other books have timeless information, or they have some historical value.

The authors have used their personal experience, and these programs have been developed using techniques and resources that work well in their libraries. This book offers quick tips on publicity, Websites, and other resources to assist the librarian in planning. Both veteran and novice librarians will find many ideas to make fashion programs rewarding and fun.

Each program addresses the forty developmental assets which have been identified by the Search Institute. These are the most frequent assets that are addressed in the programs.

- Youth as Resources: Young people are given useful roles in the community.
- Adult Role Models: Parent(s) and other adults model positive, responsible behavior.
- Youth programs: A young person spends three or more hours a week in sports, clubs, or organizations at school and/or in community organizations.
- Reading for pleasure: A young person reads for pleasure three or more hours per week.
- Caring: A young person places high value on helping other people.
- Responsibility: A young person accepts and takes personal responsibility.
- Self-esteem: A young person reports having a high self-esteem.
- Positive View of Personal Future: A young person is optimistic about her or his personal future.

These assets represent the relationships, opportunities, and personal qualities that young people need to avoid risks and to thrive. For more information about Search Institute and the forty developmental assets, visit their website at http://www.search-institute.org. After looking at the full list of developmental assets, you may find creative ways to incorporate them into your programming.

All of the programs have the same basic outline. Because it would be repetitive to present each item in this outline for each individual program, please plan to refer to the outline when planning individual programs. If a response is missing, you can use the items here to fill in the gap. If the item is extremely important in planning the individual programs, some of this information may be repeated in the chapter within the outline there.

Information in the main part of this book is sometimes supplemented with information, forms, handouts, and other items found in the appendixes of the book. These are often brief examples, and you will need to add your own trivia questions, pictures and explanations, or other items to each list.

OUTLINE FOR ALL PROGRAMS

The outline below is the basic format for all programs. You will be referred back to this outline format and content frequently in describing specific programs.

I.   Program Title:

Try to make the title exciting and fun while at the same time expressing what the program is about. Current fads and pop culture are great ways to get ideas for titles. For example, consider Upcycle instead of Recycle, and Old School for Vintage programs.

II.   About the Program:

A. Goals and Objectives Statement:

You need to write a goals and objectives statement for the program, including the why and the what for the program and decide the outcomes that are expected to benefit the library and the 'tweens and teens.

B. Address the Developmental Assets:

You will need to include what you have available in your library in staff, facilities, and collection as you prepare your goals and objectives. These should help you address what you need to accomplish.

III.   Participants:

A. Space:

If space is a challenge, take registration with a limited number. If the space will hold twenty, you might want to take twenty-five to thirty names, knowing that teens will forget or will have a conflict and not be able to come.

B. Encouraging Participation:

Emails, calls, and texting are great ways to remind teens about programs. Teenagers prefer texting as a way to communicate with you and any other teen librarians. Facebook and other social networking websites, like Twitter, are additional ways to communicate with teenagers.

IV.   Program Length:

A. Shorter Programs:

These will be between 1½ and 2 hours, but consider the number of teenagers who may attend the program.

B. Longer Programs:

Fairs, bazaars, and other programs with multiple activities may be half to full day events.

V.   Publicity:

Publicity is another important aspect to program planning. Publicity is more than a flyer posted in the teen area. While flyers are just one aspect of promoting the library and library programs, they can be effective if they can be posted in school libraries and other community places (churches and recreation areas, among others). Flyers are the back-bone of publicity.

A. Flyers:

1. Creating flyers: These need to be interesting and exciting. All flyers should be as professional as possible. Graphic programs on your computer make professional flyers possible for all-sized libraries.
2. Timing for flyers: All flyers should be up at least one month before the program.
3. Branding your program: If the library is branded, try to establish a 'tween and teen brand that will identify with both the library and your programs for teenagers.
4. Accuracy in flyers: Double check all flyers for correct spelling, dates, and times. Have another person proofread flyers before printing them. It takes some time between creation and proofreading to really spot errors.
5. Posting flyers: In your library, post flyers throughout, at the circulation desk and other appropriate locations in the library. Don't restrict flyers to just the teen area. This gives maximum exposure to the program. Place objects and books related to the theme of the program next to the flyer to draw attention to the flyer.
6. When working with community partners, include them in the publicity. Have them post flyers, and if possible create a display to highlight the program.
7. Get permission from the schools to post flyers in the schools, either in a central location or in the library.

B. Other Means of Creating Publicity:

For your programs in the teen department, include creating bookmarks to send home with parents and teens. You can also make very good use of your library's webpage to generate publicity.

1. Bookmarks: Do something different when you create a bookmark with the information on the front. Depending on the design of the bookmark, there may not be room for much information on the front. Use a teaser phrase, and then on the back give the basic information. Include a bibliography of books about the subject. Be sure these books are prominently displayed at the circulation desk for all patrons of the library. A teacher, another relative, a neighbor, or almost anyone who knows a teenager might pick up the bookmark to share.
2. Website or other Web 2.0 tools:
    a. Be sure the program is on the library's website, blog, Facebook page, and any other social networking sites.
    b. On the library's website have a short article about the subject of a program, for example, Vintage Fashion. In the article mention the program. Include pic-

tures of book jackets of six or eight titles on the subject from the collection. Check out St. Louis Public Library, the "Lure of Vintage Fashion," and then see pictures of eight book jackets in their collection at http://www.slpl.org/slpl/interests/article240118279.asp.

3. News Releases: Prepare news releases; these often need a long lead time. Contact newspapers and other media for their lead times.

4. Announcements at local schools: Many schools have an announcement system. Contact the school to see if the principal or the school librarian would be willing to announce your local library program. A good working relationship with local school librarians can often be a helpful way to get word out at the school.

5. Displays in the Teen Area:

   a. Create a display of books in the teen area, highlighting the topic of the program. Be sure to clean any book jackets before putting them on display. Keep some books for the day of the program.

   b. Have flyers, related bookmarks, and a sample of the craft, if there is one, that will be created at the program near the display so teens will pick them up to take home.

   c. Use an object that relates to the theme of the program next to the flyers, the bookmarks, and the book. If you are promoting a prom program dress, a mannequin in a prom dress could be standing next to the flyer.

   d. At the program, have a display of books for teens to check out. Be sure to have a sign next to the display that encourages teens to check out the books.

   e. Don't forget to include other library materials such as DVDs, CDs, and magazines that tie in with the program theme.

VI. Collections:

Programs are not only to entertain and give teens information but also to encourage teens to check out books and other items and to become lifelong library users and supporters. Display a variety of resources even if their titles are not all closely related to the theme. It would be an excellent time to feature the new titles in the library collection.

A. Evaluate the Collection:

1. As part of the planning process, evaluate the collection in the areas that programs are being planned. Make sure titles are current and the materials are in good condition.

2. Depending on the ordering process in your library, it may be necessary to order materials for programs three to four months prior to a program.

3. Think about the entire collection, including nonfiction, fiction, DVDs, CDs, and any other format in your young adult collection.

4. Magazines are very important. When planning fashion programs, consider adding fashion titles to the magazine collection. You might want to ask the Friends of the Library for funds to add one or two magazine titles of popular fashion-related magazines.

5. Teen magazines are consistently well used and get trashed very quickly. Having a couple of extra copies of very popular titles is a good idea.

6. Keep discarded fashion magazines for future craft projects.
7. Since nonfiction titles about proms are difficult to find, consider purchasing the special prom-related magazines as they come out.
8. In order to have plenty of magazines for craft programs, ask teens to donate any unwanted magazines to the library. If you are soliciting unwanted teen magazines, communicate this with the staff so they are aware that magazines are being collected and know where to put them. To have the magazines available for programs, keep a basket in the teen area for donations. Remove donated magazines regularly and store in the work room so that magazines will be available for programs.

VII. Craft Supplies:

A. Getting Donations:

1. In the spirit of recycling, put a basket at the circulation desk, reference desk, or in the teen area, asking customers to donate unwanted craft supplies. Post this request on the home page, blog, or other Internet sites. If specific types of materials are needed, put up a special notice several weeks before the program asking for the type of material that is needed.
2. To make craft programs "boy friendly," have a backup craft that would interest guys. For example, make duct tape wallets. Also, have material such as iron-on transfers or printed-out images from the Internet that would appeal to boys. You need to have big safety pins, chains, and anything tough-looking available for the guys. Try making your own transfers using freezer paper. For a tutorial on this project, check out: http://www.frugalupstate.com/crafts-diy/diy-freezer-paper-fabric-stencils/.
3. If the attendance for programs is small, consider searching craft and fabric stores for kits that have all of the supplies available in one box; usually these will have enough materials for up to six or eight teens.
4. Try to incorporate materials that are readily available in libraries, such as old newspapers, discarded magazines, old books, and even discarded microfilm.
5. For all craft projects have copies of the instructions available for teens to take with them to encourage them to continue to explore crafting.
6. Have labeled boxes for each type of craft material. This makes it easy to find items when setting up and, when cleaning up, store any materials that can be used in a new program.

VIII. Evaluation:

Every program needs an evaluation form to determine its success and to point out any failures so that they may be corrected in the planning before this program is repeated or before other programs are offered. If you have stated objectives for the program, evaluation becomes much simpler. If your objective is to encourage fifteen teenagers to come to your program, you can count the participants, and if you have fifteen, you will have succeeded. If you do not have fifteen, you need to find out what you need to do to encourage more to attend. Sometimes you simply need to ask those who are there where or how they found out about the program and then increase the publicity in those areas. If you have fifty and you are unprepared, this will indicate a need for an RSVP or some other way to anticipate the crowd so you can move to a larger location if you repeat the program. You might even need to offer it two or three evenings in one week if the teens seem to be really interested in the program.

The evaluation should serve not only to gain feedback from that session but also to provide ideas to help plan future programs and to design future evaluation forms to test your success. Decide what you will need to know to test the success of your program. Samples of two "Evaluation Templates" are shown below. The first is for the librarian or a staff member to complete. The second is for the participants in the event.

Evaluation Templates

For the librarian:

Name of program:	Date of program:
Number of participants anticipated:	Actual number in attendance:

The following was determined based upon observation, interviews, and survey form:

Participants seemed to enjoy the program?   Yes or No

Why or why not?

For the participants:

Name: (optional) _____

I learned about this program [List forms of publicity so they can put a check by each]

I enjoyed this program
_____   very much
_____   it was OK
_____   so-so
_____   not much
_____   didn't like it at all

I really liked:

This program could be improved by:

I have a library card.

A. Evaluation Steps:

1. Decide how you will collect this information.
    a. Will a simple visual analysis of smiles on faces be enough?
    b. Will it be a questionnaire for participants to complete? This is often a challenge because most will be anxious to leave with friends immediately after the program. Many times the chaos at the end of something like a style show will make it very difficult to get them interested in completing a survey form.
    c. Will you ask questions with a follow-up email to participants? This is much easier now with programs such as Survey Monkey.
    d. To whom do you need to report the information: your director, the cooperating agency, the funding source, or only yourself?

IX.   Before the Program Date:

A. Contract:

Have a programming contract that can be used for all programs that have outside speakers, either paid or free. The contract should include:

1. The name of the program
2. The date and time of the program
3. The time the speaker(s) should arrive
4. The amount of time that the speaker(s) have for the presentation
5. The amount, if the speaker will be paid, or if it is free; what they are expected to provide, and what the library will provide

B. Preparation:

Collecting any props and gathering any supplies that will be needed can be done over a period of time.

C. Actual project:

When doing a craft project, create a sample to understand how much time, and how many supplies, and tools will be needed. This allows for adjustments to be made prior to the actual program. For example, with certain crafts projects, it may be discovered that a hot glue gun is better than a glue stick.

D. Evaluation:

Prepare an evaluation that can be updated for each program.

E. Layout Plan:

Create a plan for the room set, which will make it easier for people helping set up to know how the room should be arranged. Keep in mind emergency exits, accessibility to facilities, and the flow of people.

F. Confirmation of Speakers:

A week or a couple of days before a speaker program, the librarian should contact them to confirm the program.

G. Refreshments:

Plan your refreshments ahead of time. Leave the shopping to a couple of days prior to the program.

H. Photos:

Arrange for a staff person or volunteer to take pictures. Take lots of pictures so that you can reference them for future programs. Teens will often request a program again.

X.   Day of the program:

A. Set Up the Room:

The setup will vary depending on the program, but for each program you will need:

1. A registration table and sign-in sheet. Include name, phone number, and email address for the sign in, and have flyers for the next program and the evaluation form to hand to the participants. Having activity sheets available is good for filling in the time prior to the beginning of the program. You will need to provide any supplies that might be needed.
2. A refreshments table. Leave refreshments in storage until it is time for them to be served. Have a volunteer available to watch and man the table. If you have a large group or multiple activities, a ticket may be given at the registration table for the refreshments. Have plenty of refreshments on hand.
3. A display. Provide a display of appropriate books with a sign that encourages the teens to check them out.
4. Put up any decorations. This is not always necessary and will depend on the program.
5. When you have a speaker, provide a presentation area with a dais and a bottle of water, and place table and chairs to face the dais.
6. Check to see that the microphone is on and all other electronics are working.

XI.   Planning the Program Agenda:

Your program will have a similar agenda for every program. However, you need to think about any differences that might make a change. If the library director wishes to bring greetings, that would need to be added to the agenda. If for some reason you have music, either electronic or provided by a specific group or person who is performing, that will alter your agenda.

A. Welcome To the Program: (5–10 minutes)

1. Welcome everyone to the program and make announcements, including upcoming events. Communicate with teens on their level; use language that would connect with them.
2. Talk about the program and what the teens will be expected to do.

B. Program:
Times will vary depending on the program. Each program should be at least 45 minutes.

C. Wrap Up: (5–10 minutes)

1. Thank everyone for coming.
2. Encourage them to check out books.
3. Ask them to complete an evaluation form if you have one prepared. Explain why there is a form and how it helps in planning future programs. Ask the teens to help put up chairs, pick up supplies, and throw away trash.

XII.   After the Program:

A. Complete the clean-up.

B. Add names from the sign-in sheet to your database.

C. Write a thank-you note to the speaker. Include a picture and a couple of positive comments from the teens' evaluations.

D. Read the evaluations and write a summary of the program.

E. Send your report to the appropriate people who will need to see it.

F. Post pictures on your library website or on a photo-sharing website. Posting pictures allows the participants to share the experience with friends and lets others know what they missed so they will be inspired to come to the next event.

PLANNING FOR BASIC PROGRAM TYPES

Some program types are repeated in different chapters throughout the book. The basic planning and setup are similar, and some basic information is placed here. You may be referred back to this section at other times. In this section we will also be discussing active and passive programs. Both are available to offer. Active programs often take more preplanning because they include more steps. One of the first items in an active program could be a guest speaker.

Finding Guest Speakers

When you have the opportunity to bring in the pros who know a great deal about the subject of the program, it will be helpful in building your 'tween and teen programming. For example, if you are doing a program on "personal style," you could ask a personal shopper to come in and talk about how to put outfits together. Sometimes these experts will come for no compensation, and other times you must have funds to pay them for their expenses in getting to the program and they may require an honorarium. Some may come from your local community and be pleased to demonstrate something especially if, at the end, they can advertise their product.

When you have decided you have a person in mind for a program, prepare a programming agreement for all programs, even the freebies, so that all parties are aware of expectations. Be sure to include date, time and any materials that will be provided as part of the program.

You will also need to know if they need any supplies or equipment, such as a projector or a microphone.

Know exactly what you want them to do and how much time they will have. Remind the speaker that they will be addressing teens and 'tweens and to acknowledge that they are young adults and converse with them on their level.

If they are unwilling to do the program, ask them if they can suggest anyone who might be available. They may have some very good suggestions; after all, they are the experts in their field.

Other active programs include fashion shows (which will be expanded later), swaps, fairs or bazaars, and exhibits. These will be followed by passive programs, which mean the 'tween or teen participates in the program off-site and brings the "product" into the library. Our first active program is the fashion show.

Fashion Shows

Fashion shows are one of the basics of all style programs. Two types of fashion shows are described in this book. One is where clothes are brought in for the teens to model, such as the Prom Fashion Show, and the other involves handmade clothing. It will be less likely that most libraries will have the space to offer the fashion show in-house, and librarians, if they need a larger space, must make sure they have the support of a partner within the community. Often a partner such as a service club in the community will have a meeting room large enough. If it is a program as popular as prom styles, it should draw a bigger audience. When shopkeepers lend their clothing, they will be pleased with as large audience as possible.

The second show will most likely not be as large because it will feature handmade creations during a program like the ABC (Anything But Clothing) Fashion Show, in which teens create outfits from recycled material, then model the outfit. This type of fashion show could also feature outfits made for a passive program. A fashion show can showcase fashions for a season or a special theme, for example, "Green Fashions" or "Vintage Fashions."

A fashion show where clothes are brought in for teens to model will need the following:

- A runway or a stage. Neither is necessary, but if you can have one, the runway should be red. Tape down red butcher paper for your runway. In many communities a red carpet can be rented or borrowed.
- Chairs. Place chairs along both sides of the runway. The models should be able to walk down the runway, pause at the end, turn around, and walk back.
- A public address system. The Master or Mistress of Ceremonies (MC) will need to be heard when narrating the show. The PA system will also provide the background music to set the mood.
- A program. For fashion shows with clothing provided by a store, you will want a program, with room for taking notes. If the clothing is created, a program is not necessary but would make a nice touch to the festivities.

Not only do you need someone to help you provide a larger space, but fashion shows that are showcasing clothes from a business or businesses in the community require time to develop a partnership with the businesses. This is the most time-consuming program to produce. On the other hand, a fashion show of handmade creations can be the culminating activity of a program. The teens will create the outfits and then model them. They will need to write a description for the MC. For either program you shouldn't forget the photographer.

Swaps

A swap is a program where teens bring things that they own and are tired of and shop for items that have been brought in by other teens. A swap doesn't have to be a one-for-one exchange, but can instead be a shopping experience. Because teens will be bringing in clothes to give away and hopefully bringing home new items, it would be advisable to require a signed permission slip from the parents before allowing a teen to participate. This requirement should be on all publicity. Also on the publicity, state that any remaining clothing will be donated to a charity thrift store if not taken back by the owner at the end of the program. Arrange for the charity to pick up all leftover items immediately following the program or the following day. Besides a clothes swap, a book swap is another possibility. A clothes swap will require the following, including supplies:

- Clothes racks. Borrow from anyone you can. You will need them for coats, dresses, skirts, and some blouses.
- Hangers: Check with local dry cleaners; hangers can be returned.

- Tables: Display shoes, accessories, and folded clothing, like T-shirts and sweaters, there. Sort by size and indicate the sizes on signs on the tables.
- Signs: These will be helpful for shoppers to find different types of clothing and different sizes. Note: if clothes don't have sizes on the label, put the size on each item using tags or masking tape.
- Dressing room. Your audience will need a place to dress if they are going to try on clothes.
- Full length mirrors. Two or more may not be necessary, but they would be useful.
- Shopping bags for taking home treasures.
- Volunteers: Help is critical to sort items when they are brought in and to assist with keeping the shopping area neat and organized during the sale.
- Holding area: Floor space near the sale or another area for teens to put their finds while continuing to shop. Have signs that say, "These items belong to (name)" so other teens will know that these items have been claimed.
- Hang out area: A space for refreshments, display of fashion books and magazines that may be checked out, and chairs and tables for chatting and eating.
- Trivia and word games: These should be in the hangout area and available for fun while taking a break.

Fairs or Bazaars

Fairs or bazaars are programs where a multitude of activities take place. The different activities are set up as stations where teens can move from one activity to another. If an activity doesn't interest them, they can spend more time at the ones that are of interest to them. Some of the fairs or bazaars in the book are in Chapter 2—the Prom Fair; Chapter 3—the All about Me Spa Retreat; and Chapter 4—the Jewelry Bazaar. For these activities you will need the following:

- Tables
- Signs for each of the stations
- Volunteers to help direct the teens in what is happening
- Specific supplies for the individual booths
- A passport—a small folded booklet—for the volunteers at each booth to stamp. Teens will be allowed only one turn at any booth.

Formal Exhibits

Formal exhibits give teens who have created a piece of fashion art an opportunity to display it in the library. Exhibits can be either a contest where the work is judged or only displays. The direction an exhibit takes depends on the individual librarians and the space in the library. When planning an exhibit, consider the following:

- Is the exhibit going to be judged with prizes, or is it going to be display only?
- Set some criteria for the artwork. For example: it must be original, it should have no obscene graphics or words, and there may be requirements about what can or cannot be used to create the piece. You may want to add other criteria. The dimensions of the art piece may be important depending on the space available.

- Decide if the exhibit is going to be judged with first, second, and third place ribbons or actual prizes or if it is only going to be a display. Judges can be members of the local art museum, local artists, high school art teachers, or the person in charge of the city's public art.
- Decide what the prizes will be. If a local store donates a grand prize, ask if the manager or owner will display the winning art in the store for two weeks to a month.
- Select a date for all designs to be submitted to the library; two to four weeks would be ideal.
- Designate a place to pick up any supplies that will be needed for the contest and for artwork to be turned in. The location should be on all publicity.
- Determine all the supplies that will be needed for logging in the art. These should be at the appropriate desk, and all staff should know the procedure for logging in the artwork.
- Plan to log in the artwork with the name of the teen artist, a phone number, and email address. A library card number can also be used because it has all the necessary information.
- List your publicity calendar and the spot where the information will be placed. On the publicity forms, have the date and time for the Exhibit Opening and the location, especially if it is different from the library and in another specific location.
- Prepare for the judging. Place all the art being entered into the contest in a central space for the judging, even if it will be displayed elsewhere later.
- Invite the judges to judge the submitted entries. If they have not developed criteria, you should have criteria and scoring sheets available for the judges to use.
- Decide if you are going to have an exhibit opening. If you are, you will need to plan to treat each teen's work as an art gallery would treat their artists. Host a gallery opening. Parents, grandparents, friends, and teachers love to see work that has been created by teens that they know. For the teens, there is a pride in having their work shown to the public. You can exhibit the designs in inexpensive paper frames or mount on poster board. If the works have been judged, have the judges available to award the prizes that evening. Finally, in the pattern of most exhibit openings, plan to provide refreshments of sparkling cider, cheese, crackers, and cookies or just cider and cookies.
- Offer a virtual exhibit. If you cannot host an on-site gallery opening, you can still share the exhibit with others. Take pictures of the submitted art and post on the library's social media sites. Ask the community to contribute comments and accolades on the exhibit. Hold a secondary contest on the virtual exhibit by having the community vote for their favorite piece.

Librarians who work with 'tweens and teens need to be very creative with their areas in the library. Because creating displays and exhibits is a skill that is new to us, you may want to find ways to create displays and exhibits by seeking out help from professionals working in museums, galleries, and even favorite retail stores. Ask them for advice.

Passive Program

A passive program is one in which teens do an activity on their own in the library or at home and bring back the finished project to the library. These types of programs are good in libraries that are space and staff challenged. When having a passive program, collect the teen's name and contact information to add to the database of teens. Collecting the teens' names also gives you statistical data. Several different types of passive programs are described in the book. They include the following:

- Create something at home and bring it to the library to be judged or to be displayed.
- A passive program can also be used as a promotional for an upcoming program. An example of this is in Chapter 5: SHHH! Shoes, Hats, and Hair Accessories Happenings. Another example is the Rotten Sneaker Contest, which can be a promotional activity for the Transform Your Sneaker program. Or it can be a stand-alone contest.
- Another passive program is a trivia or scavenger hunt. This is one of the simplest programs. Teens are challenged to answer questions or find different objects. The answer sheets or the objects are turned in. The winner is determined by the number of correct answers, the date, and the time the answer sheet was turned in.
- "Take & Make" craft projects. Put all of the supplies needed for the project in a baggie along with the instructions. Teens can pick up the baggie at a designated location in the library. The craft project can be brought back to the library display, or they can take a picture of the finished project and post it on one of the library's social networking sites.

Publicity is another important aspect to passive programming and program planning. Publicity can be, as described earlier, a flyer posted in the teen area or even outside the library. Flyers are just one aspect of promoting the library and library programs. All publicity items should be as professional as possible. All of the graphic programs available today have made professional flyers and ways to create posters possible for all sizes of libraries. Web-based publicity has also been discussed earlier. However, two additional points for Web-based publicity are:

- Publicity should be on all of the library's Internet sites, homepage, Facebook page, blogs, and any other ones available to the library.
- On the teen page, try having a photo display loop of book titles along with the flyer.

Newspapers

Newspapers were also discussed earlier. However, in this instance, you should try to get someone from the newspaper to take pictures of your event, especially if it is as important as a style show with prom dresses. If you ask when you take in your press release, you may be able to get a reporter there, but, if not, ask if they would like your report of the event and the pictures you or one of your teens might take.

Craft Programs

Many of the programs in the book are craft programs, and these are very popular with teenagers. As stated earlier in the chapter, keep a basket at the circulation reference desks in the main library, as well as in the teen area, asking customers to donate unwanted craft supplies. Post this request on the home page, blog, or other Internet sites.

- If specific types of materials are needed, put up a special notice several weeks before the program asking for the type of material that is needed.
- To make craft programs "boy friendly," buy a bunch of iron-on transfers or print out images from the Internet—like skull and crossbones, sports memorabilia, etc.

Because these are designed to bring teens into the library, you are, at all times, aware of the need to get these teens to "join" the library by getting a library card. This should be mentioned at some point in every program with the most effective time at the beginning of the session. You could put a line at the bottom of each flyer: "Sign up for a library card while you are in the library." This is their start to a lifetime of learning and use of their public library.

Welcome to the world of fashion; "Teens Have Style!" at the Library. What will your style be? The programs suggested are ideas to get the creative juices flowing. Many of the programs can be modified to fit into another program. Take the ideas and make them work for any library. Have fun, enjoy, and create special experiences for the teenagers in the communities you serve.

Share your creative ideas on our Pinterest site: http://pinterest.com/teenshavestyle. We look forward to seeing your creative ideas.

1

Fashionistas

It is healthy for teens to be able to express their personalities, and fashion is one of the ways to do this. Being able to express themselves through fashion and style allows teens to feel comfortable with their self-image. Not all teens are able to express their personalities in the fashions they would like to choose. Peer pressure is one of the reasons many teens follow the fast-changing trends, which may seem to their parents and other adults as ridiculous, at the least, and destructive when it seems to draw unwelcome attention to their children. Teen don't want to be ridiculed or feel that they aren't in with the crowd. Movies and television are also sources for many of the teen fashion trends. Library programs allow teens to experiment with different looks and styles without investing in expensive clothes.

ACTIVE PROGRAMS

What Is Your Style?

About the program:

Teens, especially 'tweens, who are just starting to develop their own style and to shop by themselves, are often not sure what their style is; they don't know how to put together outfits, find what they like, and know what looks good on them. "What is Your Style?" will give teens information on these skills:

- How to analyze their interest to develop a style
- How to analyze what's in their closet and to use what they already have to put together outfits
- How to shop for items that will extend what is already in their closet
- Different fashion terms (use Appendix A "Fashion Terms" as a handout)

During the program the teens will create an inspiration board. They will have time to clip favorite fashions to display on their inspiration board. This exercise will help them to discover their fashion style.

Suggested number of participants: Unlimited

Suggested program length: 1½–2 hours

Publicity: Flyers and others (see the Introduction)

<u>Evaluation</u>: Because this program can be more labor intensive and may also require more funding because you have a speaker, you need to plan your evaluation carefully. Will you have a questionnaire for participants to complete? This is often a challenge because most will be anxious to leave with friends immediately after the program. Have you collected their email addresses so you can do a follow-up email to participants?

<u>Before the program date</u>:

- Contact local buyers or personal shoppers from local stores where teens shop to talk about what goes into making an outfit. Ask them to bring several outfits to demonstrate how a few basic pieces can be mixed and matched and how adding accessories can help create different looks.
- Decide if you need a speaker for this program.
- Consider bringing in friends or staff members who have a good sense of fashion to present if a professional is unavailable.
- Prepare to create the inspiration board.

Inspiration Board:
  Preparation
  Supplies for the inspiration board

  - 12 x 12 x 1 inch Styrofoam board (cork or other available materials can be used) for each person
  - 14 x 14 inch piece of fabric to cover the board
  - Hot glue or fabric glue for gluing the fabric together
  - 12–18 inches of ribbon to attach to the Styrofoam as a hanger
  - Old fashion magazines and catalogs with fashion photographs that can be cut out and added to the board

Instructions for making the board

  - Wrap the Styrofoam with the fabric like a package; glue the fabric where it meets.
  - Glue the ribbon to the top of the board.
  - Additional ribbon or other decorations can be used on the board.

Other projects to be considered with this themed program are shown below.

Room Decorations:

- To inspire teens, print out quotations from famous fashion designers and post around the room. (The quotations could be used for other fashion programs, such as a fashion show and vintage fashion programs.)
- Have a Trivia handout for teens to work on about the people whose quotations are featured. (See Appendix B "Fashion Quotations," Appendix C "Fashion Designers Trivia Quiz," or Appendix E "Fashion Match Up.")

<u>Day of the program</u>:

- Speaker: About 30 minutes
- Activities:
    ○ Take quiz on determining what the teen's style is. (See Appendix D "Personal Style.") Once the teens have determined their style, they can create an inspiration board. The "inspiration board" will continue to help them develop their style.
    ○ Once the "inspiration board" is finished, the teens can then go through magazines, ads, and catalogs and cut out items that they would like to add to their wardrobe. These pictures will give them inspiration for the next shopping trip.
    ○ Make a decorative hanger to hang clothes on.

Decorative hanger

Supplies for decorative hangers

- Plastic hangers
- Plastic shopping bags—the number of shopping bags per hanger will depend on how much padding is wanted
- Tape
- 4½ yards of 1½ inch ribbon; have a variety of colors and patterns

Instructions:

- Wrap plastic bags evenly around the hanger. The plastic bags may be cut into strips. Use short strips of tape to attach them at both ends. Cover the whole hanger except for the hook.
- Next wrap ribbon around the plastic bag padding, starting at the base of the hook, leaving a 1 foot tail extending above (you'll need this to tie a bow later). Overlap the ribbon enough to hide the plastic.
- When you get back to where you started, cut the ribbon so that you have another 1 foot tail, then tie the two ends into a tight bow.
- Instead of a bow, you can cover the hook with the ribbon. Use a hot glue gun to tack the end of the ribbon in place. For more help, visit the URL www.familyfun.go.com/crafts.

If the "inspiration board" and decorative hanger are too time consuming for one program, the decorative hanger can be packaged and given out as a take home project or used in another program. Another alternative program for the "inspiration board" is offered below.

Decorate a journal

An alternative activity for the inspiration board would be to create a style journal. The journal would be smaller than the inspiration board and could be taken with the teens on their shopping trips. Inside the girls can leave space to post pictures of clothing or outfits that they have in their closet. The adjoining page could include cut-out pictures of clothes that would go with the outfit. Teens can be encouraged to make fashion sketches in the journal.

Supplies:

- Blank journal that can be decorated with pictures cut out of magazines and decorated with colored markers.
- Old fashion magazines and catalogs with fashion photographs that can be cut out and added to the board.

Dressing for an Interview

About the program:

The program is an informational workshop to give teens the basic information they need on how to dress and act for success when interviewing for a job, scholarship, or college entrance.

Suggested number of participants: Unlimited

Suggested program length: 1 hour

Before the program date:

- Partner with a school counselor, college admissions personnel, or someone in Human Resources to participate in a panel discussion about appropriate and inappropriate behavior and clothes for interviewing.
- Develop some scenarios of what not to do and what to do when interviewing. Some suggestions are given below.
- Select several teens from the Teen Council, the high school drama class, or the library to act out the scenarios that have been developed. After the interview, the panel will discuss why they would recommend or not recommend the teen for the position. You can also do interviews for entrance to college or for a scholarship. At the end of the skit and the remarks from the panel, open the discussion up to the audience.
- If a partnership is not possible, librarians and staff can prepare PowerPoint slides showing teens good and bad interviewing dress and behavior. Prepare for an open discussion afterward.
- Prepare a handout of the important things to remember when going for an interview for the teens. Include pictures on the handout for a visual reminder of the dos and don'ts.

Scenarios for Interviewing

1. Young man (John) arrives at the interview late (have the interviewer [Ms. Brock] look out the pretend door or watch). He comes hurrying in, his shirt tail is hanging half out, his hair is ruffled, and his shoe is untied. He sits down without shaking hands.

John: Hi, I'm John. I am here about the job.

Ms. Brock (standing and holding out her hand):   Hi, I'm Sue Brock, the manager of the XYZ restaurant.

John (remaining seated and not shaking her outstretched hand):   Oh, hi.

Ms. Brock: You are interested in the job as a bus boy.

John: Yeah, whatever you have.

Ms. Brock: What makes you think that you would like to work in a restaurant?

John: I really need a job to get this really cool bike.

Ms. Brock: The job requires that you work Friday nights from 6:00 to 10:00, and Saturday mornings from 6:00 a.m. to 10:00 p.m.

John: Wow, I don't know. I have to take my girlfriend out on Friday nights, and ya see, I don't get in till late and I'm not up till noon. How about I work 1:00 to 5:00 just on Saturdays? See I have to meet up with my basketball buddies at 5:00. And what does it pay?

Ms. Brock: The salary is minimum wage, $10.50 an hour.

John: Well, I don't know. I really need the money bad, and I was hoping for, like, $15.00 an hour.

Ms. Brock: Well, I am not sure that you are exactly what we are looking for. I hope you find something that suits your needs better. Thank you for coming in.

2. A young lady, Susan, is sitting in a chair in the waiting room. She is wearing a skirt, blouse, and heels. She is looking at some papers.

Mr. Brown: Hello, are you Susan Anderson?

Susan (stands):   Yes, I am Susan Anderson. Are you Mr. Brown?

Mr. Brown (holding out his hand to shake):   Yes.

They walk into his office. Inside the office, Mr. Brown gestures to a chair, and both sit down.

Mr. Brown: As you know, this job is ten hours a week doing filing, answering the phone, and doing general office work. The hours are 4:00 to 6:00 Monday to Friday and pays $10.50. Can you tell me about your experience?

Susan: I have a resume here. I have been assisting in the office at school during my free period. I answer the phone and answer questions. If I can't answer the question, I take messages. I do some filing and making photo copies when asked. I also volunteer at the Children's Discovery Museum, assisting with programs.

Mr. Brown: What do you like about your work?

Susan: I like that I am helping someone. The volunteer work at the museum is really fun because I get to play with the children and help them with craft activities or make sure they are safe on the climbing wall.

Mr. Brown: Thank you. I will be interviewing a couple more people this afternoon, and I should make a decision sometime tomorrow.

Susan: Thank you for your time. I look forward to hearing from you.

<u>Day of the program</u>:

- This program could be part of a Teen Council meeting, using it as recruitment for new members.
- Have refreshments.

Closet Swap/Trash or Treasure Party

<u>About the program</u>:

The idea is for teens to exchange clothes, shoes, and accessories for items that others have brought to swap. To go all out, set up the room like a boutique and have nice shopping bags to take home their treasures. Teens will have the opportunity to clean out their closet, get something new to wear for free, and have a good time.

<u>Suggested number of participants</u>: dependent on space, staff, and volunteers

<u>Suggested program length</u>: 2–3 hours, dependent on the number of teens participating and amount of clothing

<u>Before the program date</u>:

- Borrow clothes racks and hangers from local businesses.
- Arrange tables to be used for shoes, accessories, and folded clothing, like T-shirts and sweaters.
- Create signs for the different types of clothing and for sizes.
- If clothes don't have sizes on them, put the size on each item using tags or masking tape.
- Create a place to try on clothes and a couple of full-length mirrors. This is not necessary but would be useful.
- Stock up on bags for taking home treasures. If funds are available, provide cloth bags as a reminder of the event.

<u>Day of the program</u>:

- Everyone brings clothes they are tired of. All clothes should be clean and in good repair. If possible, have the teens bring their clothes in at least a week prior to the program. This will allow time to sort the clothes by type and by size. It should be noted on all publicity that any unwanted clothes will be donated to charity.
- On the day of the program, provide BIG signs for each type of clothing: skirts, pants, jacket, etc.
- Arrange for volunteers to help sort items when they are brought in and to assist with keeping the shopping area neat and organized.
- After the program the staff may want to pick through the leftovers for items that might be used for future programs.

Back to School Outfit or One Special Top Many Looks

About the program:

Summer reading is over, and school will be starting soon. Keep the teens coming back after summer reading programs by having a contest to win a new back-to-school outfit. Partner with a local store with fashions for teens. Ask if they will donate one gift card to the library. This program can also be done with borrowed clothes. The one special top might be an item that is purchased. An alternate idea is "The Little Black Dress," which follows this program.

Suggested number of participants: 10–30

Suggested program length: 1½ –2 hours

Before the program date:

Gather supplies:

- One very special top in a neutral color.
- A mannequin would be ideal, but if one is not available, another idea would be to hang a series of hangers together from the ceiling like a mobile. This would need to be very sturdy because teens will be taking thing off and putting things on the hangers.
- Basket of clothing, shoes, jackets, tops, jewelry, and purses, at least two or three of each item. They don't have to all be the same size but should look good with each other.

Day of the program:

Instructions:

- Divide group into teams of two to four, depending on the attendance.
- Have the first team dress the mannequin; must have a minimum of a top, bottom, and shoes.
- The second team can change two items, the top, bottom, or shoes, and add accessories.
- The next team can again change any two items and add or subtract accessories.
- After each team is finished, talk about the outfit and why it works or doesn't work.
- Take pictures of the different outfits.
- If it is possible, leave the mannequin and clothes for a few days to give other teens an opportunity to dress the mannequin.
- Post the pictures so teens can see the different outfits from the first basic outfit.
- To make this program guy friendly, have a second mannequin with guy clothes.
- If two mannequins are used, have the girls dress the girl and the guys dress the guy. After each team has dressed the mannequin, switch it around and have the guys dress the girl and the girls dress the guy. After each team has had a turn, have a discussion about the different ways girls and guys approach putting together outfits. Be sure to emphasize that there is no right or wrong outfit but many ways that a few basic pieces can be made to look different.

The Little Black Dress

About the program:

The Little Black Dress project was inspired by Sheena Matheiken, who decided to wear a little black dress for 365 days. Every day she used different accessories to make a unique outfit. See the website www.theuniformproject.com for more information.

Suggested number of participants: 10–30

Suggested program length: 1½ –2 hours

Day of the program:

- Talk about The Little Black Dress project, showing slides of the different outfits. Challenge the girls and guys to experiment with a little black dress to see what kinds of outfits they can create. To include the guys, have them create different looks with jeans and a white T-shirt. This is a very flexible program that can be used with many of the programs throughout the book. It could also be an ice breaker, a passive program, or a contests.
- Supplies:
  - Simple black dresses. For convenience you can use a black skirt or slacks and a black turtleneck or sweater; plan for one dress for every three to five teens. Have a variety of sizes available.
  - Accessories that have been provided by the staff and brought in by the teens. All the accessories will be returned at the end of the program. The accessories should include belts, scarves, hats, jewelry, vest, shoes (including boots), and accessories for the hair.
  - Set up tables for the different types of accessories.
- Instructions:
  - Divide the groups into teams, giving each team the opportunity to add two accessories, or subtract two items, until they are happy with their finished outfit.
  - Discuss what works or doesn't work about each outfit.
  - Take pictures of the different outfits to be posted on your library's Facebook page or other photo-sharing sites.
  - If possible, leave the mannequin and clothes on display for a few days to give others who missed the program in the library the opportunity to dress the mannequin.

Fashion in Art

About the program:

The idea for this program came from an article in *KiKi Magazine* (Spring 2011). Ideas for fashion come from many different sources, and one of them is art. Pull out the art books and have teens find a picture that they like, and then have them go through magazines, ads, and catalogs to see if they can put together an outfit that represents the picture. This would be an excellent program for a school librarian to have in collaboration with the art department.

<u>Suggested number of participants</u>: 10–30

<u>Suggested program length</u>: 1½ hours

<u>Day of the program</u>:

- Supplies:
  - Lots of art books, including some from the children's collection
  - Magazines, catalogs, and ads
  - Scissors and glue
  - Marking pens, colored pens
  - Colorful construction paper and white paper
- Instructions:
  - Teens look through the art books to find an art piece that they like, one that they think they can create a modern outfit that resembles it.
  - They then look through the other magazines and catalogs to find clothes and accessories for a modern take on the pictures.
  - If there are artistic teens in the group, they may want to design their own modern vision of that clothing.
- Discussion:
  - Allow twenty to thirty minutes, depending on the size of the group, to discuss which pictures they chose, why, and how they designed their modern interpretation.
- Resource:
  - *InStyle* magazine, January 2012, page 32, "Art of Fashion" and "More Art on the Runways"

Fashion Careers

<u>About the program</u>:

Fashion offers many careers in addition to modeling. Programs can be built around different aspects of the fashion industry, for example, clothing designer. Fashion magazines need graphic designers, writers, and photographers. In more rural areas, it may be difficult to find a speaker who has held or is holding a position in fashion. In that case, you may wish to try to Skype with a speaker. This program or other programs could center around the display of the clothing in a department store window or inside the department store.

<u>Suggested number of participants</u>: 30–50 or more, depending upon space availability

<u>Suggested program length</u>: 1½ hours

<u>Publicity</u>: If you have an outstanding speaker, you may want to get media coverage of this program. It should bring in an interested audience.

<u>Evaluation</u>: Survey the audience as they are leaving.

<u>Before the program date</u>: See Introduction for help in planning for a speaker.

<u>Day of the program</u>: See Introduction for setting up for the program.

PASSIVE PROGRAMS

Inspiration Board

This program is similar to the inspiration board program described in "What Is Your Style?" above.

About the program:

An inspiration board allows teens to think creatively and to be inspired about fashion. Use fashion worksheets shown below for students to create ideas to put on the inspiration board.

In or Out Worksheet

Make a list of fashion trends. Place them under "Totally In" or "Totally Out"

Totally

IN	OUT

On an 8½ sheet notebook:

Fashion Tips

Magazines are filled with many creative ideas and tips. Keep a list of your favorite fashion tips here:

<u>In library program</u>:

- Put up a large board: this could be a bulletin board or a board that is made from Styrofoam, cork, or other available material, where teens can express their creative thoughts about fashion.
- Teens are invited to post fashions that they have designed, favorite outfits, or tips on fashion.
- The rules are simple: everything must be in good taste, the comments must be polite, no "trash talking" anyone's ideas.
- Comments may be anonymous or with a first name only.
- Good times to use a fashion inspiration board would be at the end of summer when everyone is thinking about back to school clothes or before a big dance like homecoming, winter ball, or the prom.

<u>Take home program</u>:

For this program assemble inspiration board kits that teens can pick up at the library to take home.

- Supplies:
  - 12 x 12 inch Styrofoam board (or smaller if needed)
  - 14 x 14 inch piece of fabric to cover the board
  - 12–18 inches of ribbon to attach to the board as a hanger
- Include instructions for making the inspiration board in the kit.
- Ask the teen to take a picture of the finished project and post it on the library's blog, Facebook page, or photo-sharing program.

Designer Challenge

<u>About the program</u>:

Designer Challenge is a program that encourages teens to be designers. The program can be either a contest or an art exhibit. The teen with the best depiction of the theme wins. See the Introduction section on Formal Exhibits for more ideas.

Choose a theme for the challenge, for example:

- Design an ensemble for a formal dance.
- Design an outfit for the new school year.
- Design an outfit based on a picture, like a bubblegum machine or an animal.
- Design an outfit for a future year, like 2020.

Supplies:

- Silhouette of a human body, like a one-dimensional mannequin. Have both male and female silhouettes to get fashion ideas for both of them to submit the design on. Printable forms for silhouettes are available online.

Select criteria for the design:

- Determine the size: the two most common sizes would be 8½ x 11 or 11 x 17.

- Decide on the acceptable media or medium. Can they use fabric in their design?
- Decide if the design should be turned in with a frame or no frame.

Exhibit the designs:

- Exhibit in the library:
  - Find a space in your teen area where the designs can be displayed.
  - Create a voting system that allows family, friends, and library patrons to vote or comment on their favorite work.
- Virtual Exhibit:
  - Take pictures of the submitted art and post on the library's social media sites.
  - Ask the community to contribute comments and accolades on the exhibit.
  - Hold a secondary contest on the virtual exhibit by having the community vote for their favorite piece.

Creative Writing Program

About the program:

Within the fashion industry there are many occupations. Some of them include those who write, such as journalist and publicist. Many teens enjoy writing stories, songs, and poetry. The creative writing program is another program that can be a contest. It is also a program where teens can have their works published on the Internet. This would be an excellent opportunity for a school librarian to collaborate with the English department.

Instructions to teens:

- Write a short story, an essay, a song, or a poem that has a fashion theme. For example, they could write about an article of clothing that they were made to wear, loved, absolutely hated, or something that made them feel very special.
- The writing is submitted to the library blog or Facebook page.

Instructions to readers:

- On all of the library publicity, encourage the public, not only teens, to go to the library's online sites to read the writings of the teens.
- Once they have read a piece, they are encouraged to leave comments.
- Establish a way for the public to vote on the best.

For an example of an essay about a dress, check out: http://www.teenink.com/hot_topics/pride_prejudice/article/195201/Stupid-Dress/

Suggested number of participants: Unlimited

Suggested program length: 2–3 weeks, depending upon time require to post and get readers to vote

Publicity: Post flyers with the above instructions around the library and at the schools which the public library serves

Evaluation: Number of participants in the process, both writers and readers

Fashion Week

About the program:

Many communities have a Fashion Week. This is an opportunity to develop a partnership to include some Fashion Week programs at the library and to get teens involved. See the "Introduction" to this book for some ideas for Fashion Week.

Fashion Magazine Covers

About the program:

You are an intern at a fashion magazine, and you have been given the assignment to create a cover for the magazine. Choose a subject and create the cover. You might consider designating the size of the final project so that your entries are neither too large nor too small. For inspiration, look at the cover of fashion magazines. Winners will be awarded first to tenth place ribbons on the last day of the program.

Suggested number of participants: Unlimited

Suggested program length: 2–3 weeks

Publicity: Post flyers in the library and at local schools. Be sure you indicate the date the magazine covers should be returned to the library and the day the judging will be held.

Evaluation: Survey participants

Before the program date: Choose persons to evaluate the covers

Day of the program: Have students bring in their covers before or early on the day of the judging. Make sure you have sufficient space to display the entries. Your judges may wish to judge in a private space, and entries will not be displayed until after the judging.

Dress a Bear

About the program:

Have the girls bring in a stuffed animal (a bear would be the easiest) and have them design an outfit for their bear. This would be a good program for 'tweens.

Suggested number of participants: 20–30, depending upon seating at tables

Suggested program length: 1½ hours

Supplies: You will need:

- pieces of cloth
- ribbons and lace
- buttons
- scissors, needles, and thread
- Elmer's glue for those who don't want to sew anything together

Evaluation: survey

<u>Day of the program</u>: Bring out the craft supplies and set up the room with a table for supplies.

<u>After the program</u>: Have participants help you put leftover supplies away.

BIBLIOGRAPHY

Fiction

Airhead (series) by Meg Cabot, Point
Art Geeks and Prom Queens by Alyson Noël, St. Martin's Griffin, 2005
Beauty Queen by Libba Bray, Scholastic Press, 2011
Breakfast at Bloomingdales by Kristen Kemp, Point, 2009
Clique (series) by Lizi Harrison, Poppy
The Daughters by Joanna Philbin, Little Brown Books for Young People, 2010
Fashion Disaster that Changed My Life by Lauren Myracle, Puffin, New York, 2008
Fendi, Ferragamo and Fangs by Julie Kenner, Berkeley Trade, 2007
The Fold by An Na, Putnam Juvenile, 2008
Forward Adventure of Imogene (series) by Lisa Barham, Simon Pulse
Glitter Girls and the Great Fake Out by Meg Cabot, Scholastic Inc, 2010
The Good, the Fab, and the Ugly by Rachel Maude, Little Brown Books for Young Readers, 2008
Gossip Girl (series) by Cecily Von Ziegesar, Hyperion
The Interns: Truth or Fashion by Chloe Walsh, HarperTeen, 2008
It Girl (series) by Ceicly Von Ziegesar, Poppy
Modeland by Tyra Banks, Delacorte Books for Young Readers, New York, 2011
On the Runway by Melody Carlson, Zondervan, 2010 (Christian Series)
Poseur (series) by Rachel Maude, Poppy
Reflections of a Tomboy Princess by Michelle Kimberley, Universe, 2006
Sequins, Secrets and Silver Linings by Sophia Bennett, Chicken House, 2011
Survival of the Fiercest: A Sloane Sisters Novel by Anne Carey, HarperTeen, 2009

Nonfiction

America's Next Top Model: Fierce Guide to Life: The Ultimate Source of Beauty, Fashion, and Model Behavior by J.E. Bright, Universe Publishing, 2009
Asian Faces: The Essential Beauty and Make-up Guide for Asian Women by Taylor Chang-Babaran, Perigee Trade, 2007
Born Beautiful: The African American Teenager's Complete Beauty Guide by Alfred Fornay, Wiley, 2002
Classy: Exceptional Advice for the Extremely Modern Lady by Derek Blasberg, Penguin Books, 2010
Cosmo Girl! Make It Yourself, 50 Fun and Funky Projects by the editors of Cosmos
87 Ways to Throw a Killer Party by Melissa Daly, Zest Books, 2011
Famous Fashion Designers (series) by various authors, Chelsea
Fashion 101: A Crash Course in Clothing by Erika Stalder, Zest Books, 2008
Fashioned by Faith by Rachel Lee Carter, Thomas Nelson, 2011
Harper's Bazaar Fashion: Your Guide to Personal Style by Lisa Armstrong, Hearst Books, 2010
Hijas Americanas: Beauty, Body Image, and Growing Up Latino by Rosie Molinary, Seal Press, 2007
How to be a Teen Fashionista: Put Together the Hottest Outfits and Accessories—On Any Budget by Chase Koopersmith, Fair Winds, 2005

How to Draw Cool Fashions by Kathryn Clay, Snap Books, 2009
I Spy DYI by Janet Radosevich, Potter Craft, 2012
Injeaniuos by Lauren Greene, Watson-Guptilly, 2007
Injeanuity, 52 Ways to DIY Denim by Ellen Warwick and Bernice Lum, Kids Can Press, 2006
My Look: A Guide to Fashion & Style by Marlene Wallach, Simon and Schuster Children's Publishing, 2009
Nina Garcia's Look Book: What to Wear for Every Occasion by Nina Garcia, Voice, 2010
Passion for Fashion: Careers in Style by Jeanne Baker, Tundra Books, 2008
Profiles in Fashion (series) by Morgan Reynolds Publishing, 2010
Seventeen: 500 Style Tips by Emmy Faxvilla, Hearst, 2008
Seventeen: Ultimate Guide to Style: How to Find Your Perfect Look by Ann Shocker, Running Press, July, 2011
Strutting It by Jeanne Beber, Tundra Books, 2011
Style Trix for Cool Chix: The One-Stop Guide to Finding Your Perfect Look by Leann Warrick. Watson-Guptill Publications, 2005
Teen People *Celebrity Guide: Star Secrets for Gorgeous Hair, Make-up, Skin and More, Teen People,* 2005
The Teen Vogue Handbook: An Insider's Guide to Careers in Fashion, 2009
Where I Belong by Gillian Cross, Holiday House, 2011

Resources for Librarians

America's Next Top Model: Deluxe Handbook, Modern Publishing
    This title is available on Amazon and eBay in paperback.
Designer Doodles: Over 100 Designs to Complete and Create by Nellie Ryan, RP/Kids, Philadelphia, 2009
    Good resource for librarians. Combine this with *My Wonderful World of Fashion* to provide activities for fashion programs.
Look Book: 50 Iconic Beauties by Erika Stalder, Zest Books, 2011
My Wonderful World of Fashion: A Book for Creating and Dreaming by Nina Chakrabarti, Laurence King Publishing, 2009
A Smart Girl's Guide to Style by Sharon Cindrich, American Girls Publishing, 2010
Sneaker Coloring Book by Henrik Klingel, Laurence King Publishers, May 2010

Websites

<u>Pinterest</u> is a great place to share ideas. Pinterest lets you organize and share all of the beautiful things you find on the Internet. Encourage teens to browse others' pinboards to discover new things and get inspiration from people who share their interest and style. http://pinterest.com/

<u>Sartorialist blog</u> is the blog of a photographer who takes candid shots of people walking around cities all over the world. This could be a fun passive program to have a blog on which teens could post pictures of people they see walking around in clothes that they like and explain what draws them to the outfits. http://www.thesartorialist.com/

2

All Dressed Up

Teenagers have events in their lives when they will need to dress up and look extra special. Homecoming, the Prom, Bar Mitzvah, Sweet Sixteen, and Quinceanera are a few examples of important events in a teen's life. You can highlight and support these events in your library though various programs, activities, and the collection. Many of the "All Dressed Up" programs are labor intensive requiring a long planning period and a large number of volunteers; these "big" programs bring many benefits.

The publicity that will be generated is a large benefit to the library. These programs promote community involvement and allow a librarian to develop partnerships with local businesses. They should draw nonlibrary teens to come to the library. Because these programs involve the community, they generate support for other library programming in the library.

PROGRAMS

Cinderella's Closet

About the program:

The purpose of Cinderella's Closet is to help teens find a new outfit for the big event. The closet offers a no-cost alternative to shopping. It promotes a "green lifestyle" by reusing gently used evening wear. One to two months prior to the program, begin to collect prom dresses, suits, shoes, and accessories. As part of the publicity, state that the dresses must be clean and in a garment bag or on a hanger. If the size is not on the dress, include the size on the hanger or garment. Some librarians have found other creative ways to increase the selection of prom attire by asking for donations from retail shops and thrift stores. Don't forget that parents may also have formal wear that is appropriate for this type of event. If teens donate items, have parents come in with them or have a signed permission slip from the parent. Please see "Introduction" for Swaps ideas.

Suggested number of participants: More than 10 and fewer than 50

Suggested program length: 2– 4 hours (program can also be held for a couple of hours throughout a specified week)

Publicity: The placement of publicity must be carefully considered in terms of the possible number of participants you can accommodate. If 50 is your top number, you need to specify that this is something that must be reserved in advance in order to have enough gowns available. It may well be that dressing a mannequin in a prom dress and placing the mannequin next to the flyers in the teen area will be all the publicity you need.

Evaluation: Because this will require a great deal of time and effort and you will probably be in collaboration with another agency for the gowns, the evaluation for the program is very important.

Before the program date:

- List of questions to consider before planning:
  - How many teens can you accommodate?
  - Where are you going to store the items until the program? The space available will determine how far in advance you can begin collecting items.
  - Will anyone be able to select items or must they bring an item to take an item?
  - Is there an area to try on clothes? Do you have a bathroom that could be used?
  - Is there a place for a lounge area for refreshments, relaxing, and browsing prom magazines and books while waiting to try on clothes?
  - Are there volunteers and/or staff to help organize the clothes and accessories prior to the program and to help during the program?
- Supplies:
  - A camera available to take pictures
  - Two or more floor length mirrors
  - Hanging racks, which can be made from PVC pipe. See Appendix F for more information on how to create these hanging racks.
  - Changing area, either a restroom close by or partitions
  - One or more seamstresses may be willing to donate their time or charge a nominal fee to assist in small alterations during program.

Day of the program:

- Suggested guidelines:
  - Teens may take two gowns into the dressing room at a time.
  - When they come out, they return one or both dresses.
  - If teens are waiting to try on gowns or suits, they need to sign in with the changing room attendant, who will call their name when a dressing area is available. While they wait, they may shop for accessories or wait in the lounge area.
  - In the lounge, have refreshments, which will be restricted to this area. Tables and chairs should be available as a waiting area. Place the refreshments on the end of one table and provide some word searches and trivia questions to help pass the time. Other items on this table or additional tables should be books and magazines to browse and check out and an information table, to place the evaluation forms with a labeled container for collecting them and flyers for upcoming programs. All these are there to help make waiting easier.

After the program:

- The big job will be the cleanup and boxing up of the remaining items to be held over for next year's program or to be given to a charity thrift store.

- Write thank-you notes to all volunteers and organizations that donated supplies or clothing.

Prom Fashion Show

About the program:

A fashion show allows teens to see what fashion is available and what it looks like on a real person. A fashion show is a great opportunity to partner with local stores, such as retail stores, hair salons, and florists. See the "Introduction," page xviii for the Fashion Shows information on Prom programs.

Suggested number of participants: 10–15 models and unlimited audience

Suggested program length: 1½–2 hours

Publicity: Because you are going to hold this in a space where you can have a large audience, you need to create as much publicity as possible to make sure you have an appropriately sized audience to please the store owners who will be showing their dresses. It will certainly be of benefit to their businesses if your audience goes to their stores for their prom dresses, so you want to provide them with as wide an audience as possible. It should not be difficult to entice an audience if you publicize in advance and suggest that the attendance will be limited.

Before the program date:

At least three months prior to the fashion show, begin to get your community partners. When approaching them, be prepared with what you are asking them to commit to.

- Decide if you will need a stage or a runway for your fashion show. In many communities a red carpet can be rented or borrowed as a runway.
- Secure a public address system for the Master or Mistress of Ceremonies (MC) to narrate the show. It will also be used to provide background music to set the mood.
- Create a program of the fashion show that has information on the agenda, sponsors, and models, as well as space for taking notes.
- Gowns and tuxedos to be modeled. This may require their time in having the teen models try on the gowns before the event. Hair styling for the models, makeup, and flowers the day of the event for the models is also important. When asking for assistance, please remind people that they will be acknowledged in the program for the style show.
- Ask hair stylists and makeup artists if they will donate one of their services for a drawing.
- When seeking out door prizes, also ask some of the local restaurants and limousine companies.
- Use your Teen Advisory Group as models.

Day before the program or early the day of the program:

- Place chairs along both sides of the runway, with room for the models to walk down the runway, pause, and turn around.
- Make sure the models and MC are ready at least 30 minutes before show time.

- Have volunteers and staff in formal attire to greet the guests and hand out programs.
- Don't forget to have someone to take photographs before, during, and after the show.
- Your interviewers must be ready at the close of the show to ask questions of those in attendance.

Prom Fair

Prom night offers many different aspects of that special event. The big one is the dress, but don't forget the hair, makeup, walking in those very special shoes, flowers, and, of course, dancing. The fair is a collection of activities that can be separated into individual programs. See the "Introduction" on page xix for Fairs or Bazaars.

Suggested number of participants: 20–40

Suggested program length: half day

Before the program date (at least two months prior to the program):

- Schedule a hair stylist to demonstrate updos and special event styles.
- Schedule a makeup artist to come in and demonstrate how to put on evening makeup.
- Schedule a model to come in and show the girls how to walk in high heels.
- Two weeks prior to the program, contact the professionals and ask them what they will need for their demonstration and how they would like to have it arranged.
- When approaching these professionals, know exactly what you will be expecting of them. Explain that after the demonstration there will be stations where the girls can experiment, and you would like them to help advise and help the girls. Create a schedule of events for the day that can be posted and/or handed out to the participants.

Day of the program:

- Designate tables and post signs for each station.
- Assign volunteers to direct teens and let them know where to go next.
- Activities:
  - Begin the Fair with demonstrations by a hair stylist and makeup artist. Ask the stylist and artist to highlight updos and evening makeup. Ask a model to demonstrate the correct way to walk in high heels. Then it's hands-on time.
- Hands-on Stations:
  - Hair station:
    » Experimenting with creating a special hairstyle. Have a hair stylist available to assist the girls.
  - Hair Accessories:
    » Create Flower Headbands
      * Supplies:
        · Plastic headbands
        · Hot glue and gun
        · Craft ribbons
        · Silk flowers
        · Fabric paint
        · Glitter

- * Instructions:
  - Apply a dab of hot glue to one end of the plastic headband. While the glue is still wet, attach the end of the craft ribbon to it and press down firmly.
  - Wrap the ribbon tightly around the headband until it reaches the other end.
  - Apply a dab of hot glue to the other end of the headband, and press the ribbon down firmly. Cut off any excess ribbon.
  - Cut the stem off of the silk flower.
  - Use the hot glue gun to adhere the base of the flower onto one side of the headband.
  - Carefully paint small designs onto the flower, using the craft paint. Small polka dots and stripes are easy designs that will make the flower stand out. You may choose to alternate petals so that your flower is two different colors.
  - Instead of paint you may wish to put small amounts of glue to the tips of the flowers and sprinkle with glitter.
- o Rhinestone Headband:
  - » Supplies:
    - * Thin plastic headband
    - * Thin craft ribbon. In the publicity ask teens to bring thin craft ribbon in the color of their dress. Have some ribbon on hand for those who forget.
    - * Hot glue and gun
    - * Small craft rhinestones
  - » Instructions:
    - * Apply a dab of hot glue to one end of the plastic headband. Attach the end of the craft ribbon to it, and press it down firmly.
    - * Wrap the ribbon tightly around the headband until it reaches the other end.
    - * Apply a dab of hot glue to the other end of the headband, and press the ribbon down firmly. Cut off any excess ribbon.
    - * One at a time, apply a small dab of hot glue to the back of each craft rhinestone.
    - * Before the glue has time to dry, quickly press the rhinestones onto the headband starting at the left side of the headband and working your way to the right side of the headband.
- o Pretty Gemstone Pins:
  - » Supplies:
    - * Large bobby pins
    - * One-inch felt circles
    - * Colored craft gems
    - * Hot glue and gun
  - » Instructions:
    - * Apply a dab of hot glue onto the end of each bobby pin.
    - * Quickly press the center of one felt circle onto the glue and each pin.
    - * Apply a small dab of hot glue onto the back of each craft gem, and press them onto the felt circle.
    - * When you are done, none of the original felt will be showing, and you will be left with a vibrant gemstone pin.

- Makeup Station:
  - Have makeup that the girls can use to practice applying evening makeup.
    - » Supplies:
      - * Cotton balls
      - * Q-tips
      - * Mirrors
      - * Baby wipes
      - * Makeup, especially eye shadow, and don't forget the glitter makeup
  - Cozy Socks for Tired Feet:
    - » Supplies:
      - * Ballet slippers or slipper socks
      - * Embellishments, ribbons, gemstones, small silk flower in multiple colors
      - * Hot glue and guns
    - » Instructions:
      - * Embellish the ballet slippers or slipper socks to coordinate with the other prom accessories.

OTHER PROGRAM IDEAS

Dance Lessons

About the program:

Teach teens how to be confident on the dance floor. This would be an excellent opportunity to involve the guys, who might be a little concerned about this part of the event.

Contact a local dance studio and ask for their participation in this program. They may offer to have the program at their location. Ask the Teen Council to help provide the music so that you have the type of music that will be played at the prom.

Encourage the teens to wear the shoes that they will be wearing to the prom so that they can get comfortable dancing in high heels for the girls. Don't forget the guys will be wearing dress shoes and these are much different from wearing sneakers for an evening.

Glitz up Your Shoes

A new pair of shoes (or a new look on a used pair of shoes) can make any outfit special. Check out the chapter on shoes for ideas on how to transform tennis shoes into a new pair of prom worthy shoes.

PASSIVE PROGRAMS

Countdown to the Prom

As teens anxiously wait for prom, have a countdown calendar to the big event in the teen area. On different days have different ideas of things teens can be doing to get ready for the program. Don't forget to put these ideas on the library's teen page. Everyone needs some down time, so include things like "read a book" or "enjoy a prom magazine from the library."

Publicity:

Create a bookmark to promote books about proms.

Dress or Suit Exchange (see Cinderella's Closet)

About the program:

The idea behind this program is similar to Cinderella's Closet but won't require you to find additional clothing immediately before the event, but you will have collected them at another time and then have them stored for later distribution and returned or swapped. Collect dresses, suits, shoes, and accessories and keep them stored in an area of the library. Teens come in, make a selection, and take them home and return them. The items can be exchanged if that works.

Dressing the Part: Prom Inspirations

About the program:

Use your inspiration board (see Chapter 1) for a prom wish list. Have stacks of prom magazines or old teen fashion magazines. Teens can tear pictures of all things "prom" that they can attach to the board. These pictures could be used to create a look or to give inspiration about what to do on the big night.

Publicity: Use one of the ideas above for publicity, and dress a mannequin in a prom dress and place it near the flyers for the program in the teen area. Create a Fashion Section to display all the prom and fashion books.

BIBLIOGRAPHY

Fiction

The Anti-Prom by Abby McDonald, Candlewick, 2011

Art Geeks and Prom Queens by Alyson Noël, St. Martin's Griffin, 2005

Estrella's Quinceanera by Alegria Marlin, Simon & Schuster Children's Publishing, 2007

Fat Hoochie Prom Queen by Nico Medina, Simon Pulse, 2008

Hell by Stephanie Meyer, HarperTeen, 2010

Homecoming Queen (Carter House Girls Book 3) by Melody Carlson, Zonderkidz, 2008

How I Created My Perfect Prom Date by Todd Strasser. Simon Pulse, 2008

Katy's Homecoming by Kim Sawyer, Zondervan, 2011

Prom by Laurie Anderson, Puffin, 2006

Prom and Prejudice by Elizabeth Eulberg, Point, 2011

Prom Anonymous by Blake Nelson, Speak, 2007

Prom Crasher by Erin Downing, Simon Pulse, 2007

Prom Dates from Hell by Rosemary Clement-Moore, Delacorte Books for Young Readers, 2008

Prom Kings and Drama Queens by Dorian Cirrone, HarperTeen, 2008

Prom Queen Geeks by Laura Preble, Berkley Trade, 2008

Prom Season: Three Novels by Elizabeth Craft, Laurel Leaf, 2007

Top Ten Uses for an Unworn Prom Dress by Tina Ferraro, Delacorte Books for Young Readers, 2007

Truth about My Bat Mitzvah by Nora Baskin, Simon & Schuster, 2010

21 Proms by David Levithnan, Scholastic Paperbacks, 2007

We are SO Crashing Your Bat Mitzvah! by Fiona Rosenbloom, Hyperion, 2008

Will Work for Prom Dress by Aimee Ferris, EgmontUSA, 2011
You are So not Invited to my BatMitzvah! by Fiona Rosenbloom, Hyperion, 2007

Nonfiction

Very few nonfiction books have as a theme the big events in teens' lives. Below are a few titles on this big event. Many of the teen magazines come out with special prom editions. Save some of the periodical budget to purchase these as they appear in the stores, or ask the Friends' group to purchase them for the library. Have more than one copy of each available.

Mitzvah Chic: How to Host a Meaningful, Fun, Drop-Dead Gorgeous Bar or Bat Mitzvah by Gail Anthony, Fireside, 2006
Once Upon a Quinceanera by Julia Alvarez, Plume, 2008
Prom and Party Etiquette by Cindy Post Sinning, Collins, 2010
Quinceanera Connection: Your Dream Celebration on Any Budget by Priscilla Mills, American Treasures Library, 2007

Resources for Librarians:

School Library Journal, March 18, 2009, has ideas for prom events held in a public library. One of the libraries featured in the article is the Livonia Public Library in Michigan. Photos of the dresses can be seen on Flicker: Livonia Prom Dress Exchange Photostream. The local Livona newspaper, *Hometown Life*, had an article in the February 24, 2011 edition.

Program Recognitions:

See the flyer for "Prom Makeovers" at the Napoleon Branch Library, Jackson District Library, Napoleon, MI, http://www.myjdl.com/node/7583.

Operation Prom Dress is a partnership between San Jose Public Library and Vice Mayor Madison Nguyen to offer new or gently used prom dresses for free. This program includes free dry cleaning and a raffle for hair and makeup sessions. For information on this program, check out: http://www.sanjoseca.gov/district7/PDF/Prom%20Dress%20Drive%202011%20Donation%20Flyer.pdf.

3

Pamper Yourself

When girls enter middle school and high school, they begin to think about how they look, and they become concerned about hygiene because of the changes they are experiencing in their bodies and especially the changes in their skin. With their parents' approval, they will want to begin wearing makeup and taking responsibility for their own hair care. While many have mothers, sisters, or another relative they can trust or someone close to them for guidance, other teens won't be so lucky and will be forced to gather information from magazines, television, movies, and peers.

The teen librarian can use this interest and need to provide programs for teens and 'tweens about makeup, hygiene, skin care, and hair care. Programs offer teens opportunities to learn from experts and to practice what they have learned.

Remember to take time to update the materials on beauty in the library. Teens are really turned off if the hairstyles in books are very dated. The programs that follow will help you make those plans.

PROGRAMS

All about Me

About the program:

Young women love to be pampered and to look good. All about Me is helping them learn how to pamper themselves. What you title your programs and how you advertise them probably depends upon the time of day you are scheduling the program. You can call your program Girl's Night Out if you have it in the evening. The program could also be offered on a Saturday afternoon, making it an Afternoon at the Spa. Your choice of program is the first step. You will then need to decide how many beauty ideas you will cover. An all-inclusive spa program may offer a variety, while a less complicated program may focus on only one topic, such as hairstyling.

Having a spa event requires a lot of planning, setup, and cleanup. If you love the idea but it seems too overwhelming, break it into small parts and do only a couple of stations. Because the spa program will take longer than a typical program, it is covered in more depth below. Your other programs may feature only one speaker rather than several and may not require as much time, but they will require the same type of preparation.

<u>Suggested number of participants</u>: 20–30

<u>Suggested program length</u>: 2–3 hours

<u>Publicity</u>: This program requires a great deal of planning time, and it also relies on speakers who will probably be donating their time, so you will need to have carefully planned publicity that will bring in the number you want. Consider having teens register for this event to prepare and staff appropriately.

<u>Before the program date</u>:
- Publicity:
  - Because a spa program will require the assistance of volunteers, start planning a spa program at least two to three months before the program.
    - » Decide how many speakers you are going to invite and how many stations you can accommodate.
    - » Invite professionals in reflexology, hairstyling, nails (manicurists and pedicurists), and makeup to talk about their areas of expertise. Give the speakers twenty minutes to talk about their areas and to demonstrate on one or two of the teens. After the demonstrations, the girls will have an opportunity to visit the various stations that have been set up to practice what has been demonstrated. They can practice on themselves or pair them up so they can practice on each other. Choose ideas for stations.
    - » Contact local cosmetology schools for students to help with the program.
    - » Ideas for stations are the following topics:
      - * Manicures
      - * Pedicures
      - * Reflexology
      - * Makeup
      - * Potions and Lotions
      - * Decorating Containers for Potions and Lotions
      - * Spa Bag
      - * Bling for Your Tootsies
  - Consider having permission slips for parents to sign because the girls will be putting makeup and lotions on their hands, face, and feet. If you are going to require permission slips, be sure that this is clearly stated in all the publicity that goes out to the public, both hard copies and electronic.

<u>Craft Supplies</u>:
- See also the supplies needed for the different spa stations below.

<u>Day of the program</u>:
- Setup will take time. You will want the space to be relaxing and have a spa vibe. The mood can be achieved by dimming the lights and playing soft meditative music. Have comfortable chairs or pillows for relaxing and browsing through books and magazines while enjoying refreshments and waiting.

- Some stations will need bowls or buckets of water. To protect the flooring, put down plastic tarps. A large supply of towels will also be needed, and you may want to ask teens to bring one or more with them. If a teen is supposed to bring towels, be sure that is stated in the publicity, and you will need to have extra towels in case a participant forgets to bring towels.
- Stations:
  - Reflexology: Ask the consultant for a reflexology pressure point chart with copies to be given to the teens. As they work with a partner and with the aid of the reflexologies, let the teens experiment giving themselves a treatment.
  - Hairstyling
  - Manicures and Pedicures: Depending on the number of girls, there may only be time for either a manicure or a pedicure.
  - Toe Charms: This can provide an activity for those who do not want a pedicure or if there isn't time for every participant to have a pedicure.
    - » Supplies:
      - * Small bottles of nail polish
      - * Foot lotions
      - * Towels to put under the foot soakers
      - * Tubs with water, foot soakers
      - * Scrubbers
      - * Manicuring supplies (clippers, emery boards, tweezers, cuticle trimmers, etc.)
      - * Flip flops (You will need to tell the participants, in the publicity, that these will be required for pedicures.)
      - * For toe charms:
        - • Invisible wire (elastic)
        - • Flat beads/small hanging charms
        - • Scissors
        - • Jewelry glue
        - • Instructions: Select one bead or charm to use for the project. Measure wire around the toe and cut two inches longer. (You will need the length to create the knot.) Thread desired bead/charm on wire. Center it and add a dab of glue to affix bead to wire. Loosely tie wire around the toe and secure wire knot. Cut excess wire.
      - * Makeup: The makeup artist will be available to talk with the teens and assist them in their application.
        - • Supplies:
          - ○ Small sample of makeup that they can use and take with them. (Ask local makeup retailers for samples.)
          - ○ Mirrors
          - ○ Cotton balls and Q-tips
          - ○ Baby wipes
      - * Potions and lotions
        - • How many potions and lotions you wish to make depends on time, number of teens you plan on attending, and budget.

- In addition to the ingredients for the potions and lotions, you will need some type of containers to put them in.
- If time permits, the teens can try facial masks. Because the mask must be left on for fifteen to twenty minutes, they are not the most practical activity for the spa program but will be good for teens to try at home. Instructions for the facial mask are in Appendix G.

* Spa Bag (packaging) Station

  After signing in and while waiting for the group to gather, participants can decorate their spa bags. These will be used to put their "treasures" in during the program. If they haven't completed their spa bag, they can finish after the speakers. Others who arrive late will make their spa bags after the speaker segment.
  - Supplies: Check local craft stores or online shops for the following:
    - Small plastic containers with lids or small white paper bags with handles (see www.beau-coup.com)
    - Glue, scissors
    - Old magazines, markers, and colored pencils
    - Labels and stickers to decorate the containers and to confirm ownership
    - Ribbon

- Speakers:
  - Depending upon the number of speakers, you may have limited time. You need at least twenty minutes for each speaker. They should demonstrate their skills on at least one teen.
- Refreshments:

  Refreshments should reflect the spa theme. Serve spa food: raw vegetables, fruit, and ice water or lemonade. If you decide to leave this theme, serve small cookies, mini muffins, or cake pops and chocolate candy.

OTHER PROGRAMS TO PAMPER

Decorated Hands: Henna

About the program:

Many cultures use body art. One of the better known is henna. Because henna is semi-permanent, get permission slips signed by parents. The book *101+ Teen Programs that Work,* by Rose Mary Honnold, Neal-Schuman Publishers, Inc., New York, 2003, has a Hehndi Tattoo and a Taste of India program with some very helpful instructions.

Before the program date:

- Find a community resource that knows the history of henna and the safety issues and is willing to lead a discussion on the various aspects of henna.
- Once there has been a discussion about henna, there will be time for putting on a design.
- Consider using temporary tattoo makeup and henna style stencils for quicker results.
- Girls will design henna art on her own hand or that of a friend.

- For girls who don't want to have their hands painted, have a printout of a hand pattern available. Select hand paper patterns from pictures or from stencils and decorate the hand with water colors or colored pencils.
- Another possibility would be to have girls design what they might have painted on their face for an athletic event.

Funky Hair or Tangled Workshop

About the program:

The Funky Hair program goes beyond the regular hairstyling and coloring. It is about all the extra ways that teens can wear their hair to express their personality. Because the program includes using spray color and gels and spiking the hair with gel, get permission slips signed by parents beforehand.

Before the program date:

Find two or more local hair stylists who are willing to come in and talk to teens about hair care and coloring, including spray-on color and gels, extensions, styles that are popular, and styles that are best for different face shapes.

- Have the hair stylists demonstrate funky styles on one or more teens, then give them an opportunity to try out some funky designs.
  ○ While some are experimenting with funky hairstyles, have other stations available.
  ○ Ask the stylist to demonstrate some of the techniques that can be done without water. Other alternatives for participants who do not want a funky hairdo are:
    » Braiding station: For this, get some wigs and a wig stand and have the hair stylist or even a mother show the girls how to do different types of braids. They can then practice on the wigs if they don't have long hair.
    » Headbands: Tie One On uses headbands made from old ties. Instructions may be found in *The Naughty Secretary Club: The Working Girl's Guide to Handmade Jewelry*, Jennifer Perkins, page 69.
    » Hair clips:
      * Supplies: Ribbon Flower Barrette/Headband, 1–2 yards of wire ribbon (depending on how large and tight you want your flower), coordinating strong thread, needle supplies
        • Instructions: Pull on the wire of one side of the ribbon to ruffle. Ruffle the entire length of your piece of ribbon. Not all wire ribbon is the same. Some are more fragile, so pull gently. Leave a few inches of wire hanging out from the ends, but clip away the rest to get it out of your way.
        To start: fold your ribbon back and forth a few times (on the side of the ribbon which you've just pulled the wire). Using quilting thread, run a stitch through the ribbon several times to secure. Start wrapping the ribbon around. Secure each wrap by stitching all the way through the layers in a star pattern. Once it is large enough to be difficult to stitch through all the layers, secure by stitching to the previous layer.

When you come to the end of the ribbon, fold the corner of ribbon back inside to hide the raw edge. Stitch into place. Cut off any excess wire hanging out of the ends.

Attach to hair clip or headband using hot glue gun.

Variations to the hair clip or headband can include attaching a pin to make a corsage to accessorize clothing or hats, adding a few feathers to each side of the flower, or gluing rhinestones on a few of the flower petals.

BIBLIOGRAPHY

Fiction

Because of Anya by Margaret Peterson Haddix, Simon & Schuster Children's Publishing, 2004
Fairest of Them All by Jan Blazamir, MTV, 2009
Golden: A Retelling of Rapunzel by Cameron Doky, Simon Pulse, 2007
My Life in Pink and Green by Lisa Greenwald, Amulet Books, 2010
Why I Let My Hair Grow Out by Maryrose Wood, Berkley Trade, 2007

Nonfiction

The Art of Mehndi: Learn the Ancient Art of Painting Hands, Ankles, and More by Jane Glicksman, Lowell House, 2000, http://www.amazon.com/Art-Mehndi-Ancient-Painting-Ankles/dp/0737304588/ref=sr_1_1?ie=UTF8&s=books&qid=1287701342&sr=1-1 - #
Ask CosmoGIRL! About Beauty: All the Answers to Your Questions about Hair, Makeup, Skin & More by the editors of *CosmoGirl*, Hearst, 2008
Beauty Basics for Teens: the Complete Skin-Care, Hair-Care and Nail Care Guide by Dianne York-Goldman, Three River Press, 2001
Bobbie Brown Rules: Fabulous Looks, Beauty Essentials, and Life Lessons by Bobbie Brown, Chronicle Books, 2010
Braiding: Easy Styles for Everyone by Jamie Rines Jones, Sterling, 2007
Crafty Girl Hair: Things to Make and Do by Jennifer Traig, Chronicle Books, 2004
Fun Fingers Fancy Feet by Jane Glickman, Lowell House, 2000
Going Natural: How to Fall in Love with Nappy Hair by Mirelle Liong-A-Kong, Sabi Wiri Inc., 2004
Great Braids: The New Way to Exciting Hair Style by Thomas Hardy, Sterling, 1997
Lauren Conrad Style by Lauren Conrad, HarperCollins, 2010
The Look Book: 50 Iconic Beauties and How to Achieve Their Signature Styles by Erika Stalder, Zest Books, 2011
Mehndi: The Timeless Art of Henna by Loretta Roome, St. Martin's Griffin, 1998
Pro Nail Care, Salon Secrets of the Professionals by Leigh Toselli, Firefly Books, 2009
Rescue Your Nails by Ji Baek, Workman Publishing Company, 2009
Seventeen: 500 Beauty Tips: Look Your Best for School, Weekend, and Parties & More! by *Seventeen* Magazine (editors), Hearst, 2009
Seventeen: How to be Gorgeous: The Ultimate Guide to Make-up, Hair and More by Elizabeth Brown, HarperTeen, 2000
Teen Beauty Secrets: Fresh, Simple, Sassy Tips for Your Perfect Look by Dane Irons, Sourcebooks Inc., 2002
Teen Make-up: Looks to Match Every Mood by Linda Masd, Watson-Guptitl, 2004

Teen People Celebrity Guide: Star Secrets for Gorgeous Hair, Make-up, Skin and More by *TeenPeople* Editor, *TeenPeople*, 2005

The Teen Vogue Handbook by *Teen Vogue*, Razorbill, 2009

Trix for Cool Chix: Easy-to-Make Lotions, Potions, and Spells to Bring out a Beautiful You by Caroline Naylor, Watson-Guptill, 2003

Using your Head and Common Scents by Lisa Schweitzer, Grosset & Dunlap, 2003

Resources for Librarians

Hair Wraps by Anne Johnson, Klutz, 1998 (spiral bound)

Nail Art by Sherrie Haab, Klutz, 2008

250 Stencil Designs from India (copyright free) by K. Prakash, Dover, 1996

4

Putting on the Bling

Personal expression is very important for teens, and jewelry is one of the most likely accessories available to teens to express themselves. Costume jewelry is one of the least expensive accessories to purchase, and it offers many different styles. The librarian can provide a jewelry program that can be as simple as stringing beads on an elastic thread to more complex techniques, thus making programs appealing to many teens. It is also possible to make it a learning event for older teens, who will be making decisions about purchasing a class ring or even considering a friendship or engagement ring for someone in their lives.

In creating costume jewelry, teens will learn basic techniques such as wire wrapping, crimping beads, and using jump rings. If you have had no experience making jewelry, you may want to work with someone who can help you learn the basics. This may be someone who owns a local store selling beads who knows how to make them into jewelry.

Your first step is to see what books you have in your library collection about making jewelry. Your jewelry program will provide an excellent opportunity to highlight all of these books. Your book display can offer instructions for jewelry projects, show pictures of finished jewelry projects, and discuss the raw materials to use in creating jewelry. The examples shown can also launch inspirations for teens.

Two current jewelry trends that teens are excited about are hardware jewelry, using items found in a hardware store, and "upcycle" jewelry, which uses found items to make trendy jewelry. Teens enjoy making jewelry items based on hot teens' books. For example, teens can make a *Twilight*-inspired bracelet or a *Hunger Games* pin. Jewelry programs appeal to both teen girls and teen boys. You may be surprised by the jewelry teenage boys create for themselves.

The first programs suggested below begin with those learning events at which your patrons learn about gems. They involve a knowledgeable jeweler who is willing to come in and talk about gems and perhaps would be willing and able to offer some career suggestions for anyone who is interested in working as a jeweler or who might want to own a jewelry store at some time. As you ask the persons to come speak to your students, it would be a good idea to explain that their role is to help those in the audience learn. Any sales pitch to come to the jewelry shop should be mentioned only at the end of the talk.

Craft projects throughout this chapter can be used to extend this program. However, this might seem anticlimactic to many who will be lost in dreams of diamonds and rubies.

ACTIVE PROGRAMS

Gems 101

<u>About the program</u>:

Your publicity will read, "Welcome to the World of Gemstones and Learn about Diamonds and Other Precious Stones." We have all heard the words diamonds, emeralds, sapphires, carets, cuts, and settings, but what do we really know about gems? This program will provide information that teens will be able to use throughout their lives. They should understand the differences between different sizes and weights of gems, the importance of the way the gem is cut, how to determine a flawed stone, and the importance of the setting for a gem. They should also learn a little about the care of their gems and perhaps a little about insuring a valuable piece of jewelry.

<u>Suggested number of participants</u>: 10–50

It may be difficult for 50 participants to see the examples unless you have some way to project the pieces of jewelry or the gems.

<u>Suggested program length</u>: 1½ hours

<u>Publicity</u>:

Because you will be anticipating a "volunteer" jeweler, your publicity should carry at least one reference to the store the jeweler represents. It can be added with a comma after the name, e.g., "John Smith, Smith's Jewels, will be our guest speaker."

<u>Craft supplies</u>:

The list for craft supplies will match the type of jewelry you will plan to have participants produce.

<u>Evaluation</u>:

This program involves speakers, and a formal survey or other form of evaluation tool should be administered to gather the value of this program for future offerings.

<u>Before the program date</u>:

- Review the Introduction for information on Finding Guest Speakers.
- Contact a jeweler who is willing to talk to teens about the world of gemstones and being a jeweler.
  - Ask the jeweler if he or she would be willing to bring some gems so the teens can have the experience of seeing gems. You may need to provide some security for this since any gem has a monetary value for what is a very small item, and losing a gem could happen easily if care is not taken to keep it safe.
  - Gather some books on gems to have for a display.
  - Create some trivia games and other word games about gems.
  - If a craft is to be included in the program, gather the supplies.

<u>Day of the program</u>:

The presentation should be between 20 and 30 minutes; allow time for questions from the teens.

- Speaker: a gemologist or jeweler

- Five-minute pop quiz. When the speaker is finished, have a five-minute pop quiz. An example is found in Appendix H, "Test Your Knowledge about Semi-precious Gems." If funds allow, present the winner with a diamond ring paperweight. These diamond ring paperweights are available on the Internet. If you have boys in your program, they may prefer a diamond ring key chain. You could also present a gift card to an accessories store in your local mall or a costume jewelry department in a store.

Jewelry 101

About the program:

Test teens' knowledge about the styles and types of jewelry. Jewelry 101 can be a stand-alone program or for a longer program, combine with Gems 101.

Suggested number of participants: 10–25

Suggested program length: 1 to 1½ hours

Craft supplies:

The list for craft supplies will match the type of jewelry you will plan to have participants produce.

Evaluation:

This program involves speakers, so a formal survey or other form of evaluation tool should be administered to gather the value of this program for future offerings.

Before the program date:

- Contact a jeweler, or a knowledgeable person who works in a department store selling jewelry, who is willing to talk to teens about the world of jewelry.
  - Ask the speaker if it would be possible to bring some sample jewelry in a variety of price ranges so the teens can have the experience of making comparisons. You may need to provide some security for this since these pieces of jewelry will have a monetary value for what is a very small item, and losing a piece of jewelry could happen easily if care is not taken to keep it safe.
  - The presentation should be between 20 and 30 minutes.
  - Gather some books on jewelry and how it accentuates fashion to have as a display.
  - Create some trivia games and other word games about jewelry.
  - If a craft is to be included in the program, gather the supplies.

Day of the program:

The presentation should be between 20 and 30 minutes and allow time for questions from the teens.

- Speaker
- Begin the craft program with the "Jewelry Trivia Quiz" in Appendix I.
- Proceed to the crafting area, where teens can chose from one or two jewelry making projects. Any of the craft projects found in this chapter will work well with this program.

All About Gems and Jewelry

About the program:

The combination of Gems 101 and Jewelry 101 programs combines the gems with artistic design to make jewelry. This program is to inform teens about the world of gems and how they are multigenerational and multicultural because people of all ages love gems and jewelry. Gems come from all over the world, and jewelry is worn in all countries for many different reasons.

Suggested number of participants: 20–50

This program will need to accommodate a larger audience if it is to include an audience of all ages rather than just teens. You might want to query your Teen Advisory Board if they want this program to be opened to more than teens.

Suggested program length: 3 hours

Craft supplies:

The list for craft supplies will match the type of jewelry you will plan to have participants produce.

Evaluation:

This program involves speakers, so a formal survey or other form of evaluation tool should be administered to gather the value of this program for future offerings.

Before the program date:

- A combined Jewelry and Gems program would include two speakers. The first could be a gemologist or jeweler to talk about gems and creating jewelry with gems. The other speaker would be someone who knows about all the different styles and types of jewelry.
- Ask both speakers to bring examples so teens visually see what the speakers are talking about.
- Explain that each speaker will have 30 minutes and time for questions and answers.
- Gather any items needed for the chosen craft.

Day of the program:

- Introduce speaker(s).
- Test the teens' knowledge of jewelry with a fun trivia contest. The trivia contest can be a paper activity as an icebreaker before a program or it can be the Numbered Chair game. See also the "Match the Type of Jewelry" in Appendix J and "Unscramble the Gems" in Appendix K.
- Participants will choose materials for the craft and create an item.

Tacky Jewelry Finds

About the program:

Tacky Jewelry Finds is a fun and relaxing program in which the teens bring in the tackiest jewelry they own that they have purchased and now no longer like or something someone has given to them. In the programming information, emphasis is placed on bringing very inexpensive pieces. Teens can trade until they leave with a new piece of tacky jewelry. This program and the next program, Holiday Jewelry Swap, would be fun programs to get teens interacting with each other.

<u>Suggested number of participants</u>: 20+

If the group is large, break into smaller groups of between 10 and 15

<u>Suggested program length</u>: 1½–2 hours

<u>Publicity</u>:

On all publicity, instruct teens to bring the tackiest piece of jewelry that they have and that they want to trade. Advise the teens to scour their jewelry boxes, their parents', or another relative's jewelry box (with their permission!) and local secondhand stores for just the right piece. Place in a plain paper lunch bag and staple shut. The idea is to be secretive about the gift.

<u>Before the program date</u>:

- Print out numbers. Print out more numbers than the number of attendees you expect, just in case you get a larger turnout than expected.
- Find some tacky jewelry, some that you have, or ask staff members to contribute or purchase. These pieces can be used for teens arriving without a piece of jewelry.
- Gather together supplies that will be needed for the activity.
  - Glue, especially fabric glue
  - Scissors
  - Needle-nose pliers
  - Various types of materials that can be added to jewelry: gems, beads, ribbon, chain, fabric, especially felt, or anything else you can think of.
  - Find two prizes. The first prize goes to the teen who ended up with the tackiest piece of jewelry. On a piece of paper, the teens will write the number of the tackiest piece. After they have repurposed their jewelry, they will again vote, this time for the best repurposed piece.

<u>Day of the program</u>:

- Tell the teens to be secretive about their jewelry. The idea is for people to not know who brought each piece of jewelry.
- If teens arrive without their jewelry in a brown paper bag, provide them with a plain paper lunch bag to stash their jewelry piece in and staple it shut.

Have chairs arranged in a circle, and once they are seated, every participant will draw a number.

<u>Jewelry exchange</u>:

- Begin with #1, who chooses and opens a gift. The next person will make a choice of opening a gift or "stealing" an already opened gift. If she steals a gift, the person with the stolen gift has an option of stealing from someone else or opening a new gift.
- A gift can only be stolen three times. You cannot steal the gift that was just stolen from you.

- Go to the next person in order and repeat. The exchange continues until every gift has been opened and the last person keeps her gift.

Repurposing the tacky jewelry:

- Once the last sack has been opened, everyone can take their tacky jewelry and go to the craft tables, where they can repurpose their treasure by adding something new or they can take away things on the piece and add something new. The only limit is the teens' imagination.
- As teens discard pieces of their tacky jewelry, you may wish to collect the discards and allow other teams to use parts of the unused jewelry.
- Take pictures of the jewelry before and after.
- Don't forget to vote again on the best repurposed piece of jewelry.

Holiday Jewelry Swap

About the program:

A jewelry swap would be a good holiday program. Start the program with an icebreaker. Invite teens to look through fashion magazines and catalogs for jewelry they would like to wear. They could cut them out the pictures and paste on paper as a holiday wish list. As they are making their wish list, they can share their finds with other teens. The teen could also discuss what she might wear with the jewelry. Spend about fifteen minutes working on the wish list. Then have a white elephant exchange. See the program Tacky Jewelry Finds for information on a jewelry or white elephant swap.

Suggested number of participants: No more than 20

The game takes a long time to finally get to that last number. If you have a large teen group, you could break them up into smaller groups.

Suggested program length: 1–1½ hours

Publicity: In your publicity, instruct teens to bring a wrapped piece of jewelry from their collection or to bring an inexpensive piece they have purchased. All pieces need to be in good condition and inexpensive. Participants should be secretive about their gifts. The idea is for no one to know who brought the gift.

Day of the program:

Begin with a short 5–10 minute introduction, welcoming teens and explaining the rules of the game. Hand each participant a number and begin the game.

- Begin with #1, who chooses and opens a gift. The next person will make a choice of opening a gift or "stealing" an already opened gift. If she steals a gift, the person with the stolen gift has an option of stealing from someone else, or opening a new gift.
- A gift can only be stolen three times. You cannot steal the gift that was just stolen from you.
- Go to the next person in order and repeat. The exchange continues until every gift has been opened and the last person keeps the gift that she has.

<u>Optional activity</u>: Jewelry Inspirations (15 minutes)

Have teens spend some time creating a holiday inspiration board that reflects their favorite jewelry styles and fashions.

- Supplies:
  - Scissors
  - Glue
  - Holiday wrapping paper, ribbons, and other embellishments
  - 11 x 14 poster board
- Instructions:
  - Cover the poster board with wrapping paper. If teens are inspired, they can embellish their boards.
  - Invite teens to look through fashion magazines and catalogs for jewelry they would like to wear.
  - Cut pictures out and paste on paper for a holiday wish list. As they are making their wish list, they can share their finds with other teens.
  - The teen could also discuss what they might wear with the jewelry.
  - Spend about 15 minutes working on the wish list. Then have a jewelry exchange or white elephant swap.

Jewelry Exchange

<u>About the program</u>:

This gives teens the opportunity to trade their slightly used jewelry items for something that other teens in the program have brought. Unlike Tacky Jewelry Finds, for this program teens are encouraged to bring something that is stylish but that they no longer wear. Teens can trade until they leave with a new piece of jewelry to update their collection. See the Introduction for the section on Swaps for more information.

<u>Suggested number of participants</u>: Limited only by space and staff time

<u>Suggested length of program</u>: 1½–2 hours

<u>Publicity</u>: On all publicity, ask teens to bring any jewelry that they are tired of so they can "shop" for something new. All pieces need to be in good condition and inexpensive.

<u>Before the program date</u>:

- Make signs for the different types of jewelry to place on the tables.
- Purchase small white bags with handles; these are available at 99 cent stores and craft stores.
- Have some extra jewelry handy if the supply runs low.

<u>Day of the program</u>:

When a teen arrives with jewelry, have her place it in the designated area. Give each teen a bag for the treasures she will find. Once they have laid out their jewelry, they are free to shop.

- Optional activity:
  - If time allows, set up a table for teens to create their own jewelry inspiration boards. Instructions can be found under the activity titled Jewelry Inspirations under the Holiday Jewelry Swap program described above.

<u>Refreshments</u>:

While teens shop and work on their jewelry inspirations, they can take a break with light refreshments.

Creating Jewelry out of Hardware

The craft projects below can be included in any of the programs in this book.

Personalized Washer Necklace

<u>About the program</u>:

A variety of current books are available to show how to make jewelry from hardware supplies; many of these ideas are easy and inexpensive. Also, the results are edgy and unique, which should appeal to teens. One craft idea is shown here, but check the books listed for many others, and you can provide the teens with various supplies and techniques. Also you can find lots of online craft communities with step-by-step tutorials.

<u>Suggested number of participants</u>: 10–30 (as you get closer to 30 participants, you will need additional staff to help teens with basic jewelry making techniques)

<u>Suggested program length</u>: 1½–2 hours

<u>Before the program date</u>:

- Supplies:
  - Washers (in varying sizes)
  - Alphabet Metal Die punches (check local hardware and crafts stores)
  - Mallet or heavy hammer
  - Leather, ribbon, or a chain to put the charm on
  - Baby wipes and permanent markers
  - Additional charms or beads for further embellishments
- Instructions:
  Note: As with other craft projects, you should create one or more so that you are certain you know how the process works. Also, you will have an example for those who need an example for them to see the final project.
  - Have a very sturdy table and a piece of metal or 2x4 lumber for pounding.
  - Pull out the letters you will be using, and put them in order. Make sure the letters are spaced and will all fit on washers.
  - Hold die on top of washer and hit it with the hammer to make the impression. You may need to hit it more than once to get a clear image. Continue with all letters.

- If you want the letters to stand out, you can color over the letters with pemanent markers and use a baby wipe to remove color from the surface of the charm so that the color is only left on the letters.
- Now just thread your "chain" of choice through the hole.

Jewelry Holder

About the program:

When craft programs are popular at your library, try offering a series of jewelry craft programs. Making a jewelry holder could be the last in the series to round out the programs. All that great jewelry will need a home. Picture frame jewelry holders and tree style holders offer a unique twist on a traditional jewelry box.

Suggested number of participants: 10–30 (if the interest is greater than the space, staff, and supplies, consider having two programs)

Suggested program length: 1–1½ hours

Picture Frame Jewelry Holder:

- Supplies:
  - Picture frames (look at dollar stores and Oriental Trading for the best buys)
  - Wire mesh (precut ahead of time to minimize sizing issues)
  - Paint, decorative fabric, paper, or even magazines
  - Decoupage; modge is one type
  - Wire cutters
  - Hot glue gun
  - Optional: several blow dryers
- Instructions:
  - Remove glass and backing from frame.
  - Choose materials to decorate frame. You can chose a combination of layering paint and papers/fabric, but keep in mind that the drying time will be extended.
  - You may need to use the blow dryer to make frame dry enough to handle.
  - Hot glue screen to the back side of frame.

For additional jewelry holders or display ideas, see Diva Displays: http://www.jewelry-display-ideas.com/diva-displays.html.

Personalized Shrinky Dink Charms

About the program:

This program is ideal for crafts. Shrinky Dink Paper will allow teens to create charms and then watch them shrink down to one-third their original size. The charms will be colorful and durable and will provide teens with original jewelry for their collection.

Suggested number of participants: No more than 20

Suggested program length: 1–1½ hours

Supplies:

- Shrinky Dink Paper (you can also use the Shrinky Dink paper for inkjets to print out images for charms)
- Permanent markers or crayons
- Scissors
- Jump rings
- Other jewelry finds
- Pliers
- Tweezers

Instructions:

- Draw each charm design idea chosen for the bracelet directly on to the Shrinky Dink material. Designs can be hand drawn or traced from pictures.
- Color in the design as desired, using markers.
- Cut out each charm design, getting as close as possible to the outside edge of the picture.
- Punch a hole in the top of the charm. Be sure to get close to the top edge without getting too close, or the opening won't hold the "O" ring properly. Make sure you punch the hole before you shrink the item.
- Preheat the oven to 325 degrees. While it heats, place oven paper on a cookie sheet before laying each charm, colored side facing up, onto the sheet.
- Put the charms into the preheated oven and watch as the Shrinky Dinks begin to shrink. This will take between one and three minutes. The charms should curl slightly as they shrink and then flatten out toward the end. If they do not flatten out properly, be sure to flatten them immediately upon removal from the oven before they begin to cool.
- If you don't have access to an oven: Another way to shrink charms is by using a heat gun. Use tweezers or a pencil to hold down the charm. Be careful: the gun does get hot.
- Place an "O" ring in each charm, and then attach them to the charm bracelet once the charms all thoroughly cool. Evenly space the charms throughout the bracelet.

More Accessories

Accessories are any small article or item of clothing carried or worn to complement a garment or outfit, including handbags, scarves, and hats. Most of the library programs are focused on jewelry, but other accessories would also make a good program.

Bag It

About the program:

All teen girls need someplace to carry the essentials of life. Purses, handbags, backpacks, or messenger bags are all words to describe a receptacle for carrying money, identification, and other small items. If the receptacle is large enough, it may also carry books and a laptop. Some purse programs can be too difficult, requiring a sewing machine but there are still programs that are possible for teen library programs. In this one, a simple cosmetic bag will be turned into a unique small purse.

<u>Suggested number of participants</u>: 10–20

<u>Suggested program length</u>: ½ to 1 hour

<u>Publicity</u>: Clearly state on all flyers and online publicity if you need for the teens to bring their own small cosmetic bags with a zipper for this project.

<u>Before the program date</u>:

- Purchase or gather supplies.
  - Supplies:
    - » Small plain cosmetic bags with zipper
    - » White plastic-coated craft wire, 24 gauge, for each purse
    - » 8mm plastic pearls (One large bag or enough to cover the wire for each purse, which will become the handle. Another idea for the handle would be a length of small chain.)
    - » Rickrack or other material to decorate the purse—for example, feathers, lace, and silk flowers. Be creative; there are other materials out there that could be used for this purse. Each purse will need at least 18 inches of trim.
    - » Large needles
    - » Old scissors
    - » Mod Podge glue
- Instructions:
  - Use a large needle or needle tool to carefully poke a hole in each side of the bag.
  - Starting from the outside, poke one end of the wire through the first hole into the inside of the purse. Twist the wire end a few times around the length of wire to secure. Clip off any extra wire.
  - String plastic pearls onto the wire to make the handle. Stop when you have about three inches of wire left.
  - Starting from the outside, poke the other end of the wire through the second hole. Twist the end around the length of wire to secure. Clip off any extra.
  - Use modge to put rickrack or other trim on the purse.
  - Carefully lay the purse on its back and let it dry overnight.

For more purse ideas, see *Hip Handbag Book* by Sherri Haab, page 30, Potter Craft, 2004.

Scarves
All Tied Up

<u>About the program</u>:

Scarves are a popular accessory because they are versatile and can be inexpensive. Many teens may be unsure how to wear scarves. Teen guys are often seen wearing scarves, especially in the winter with their coats. This program will help teens be more comfortable experimenting with scarves after the program.

<u>Suggested number of participants</u>: 10–25

<u>Suggested length of program</u>: 1½–2 hours

<u>Before the program date</u>:

- Find a speaker to demonstrate the many different ways to wear a scarf. Let him or her know that it should be a hands-on demonstration. After showing the teens the different ways to tie and wear a scarf, there will be time for the teens to practice. The speaker will assist the teens with their scarves. Also, tell the speaker to bring some scarves for the guys. If they can learn to tie a necktie, this would be fun for the guys.
- An option to a speaker is to show a YouTube presentation on tying a scarf. There are several, called "25 Ways to Tie a Scarf." For the guys and girls, there are YouTube videos on "How to Tie a Tie."
- Check out the YouTube video "How to Make a No Sew Fleece Scarf."

<u>Day of the program</u>:

- Tie One On is the hands-on part of the program. Teens find different types of scarves and discover how different styles of scarves can be tied and how they can be used for belts or even headbands (15 minutes). Guys can practice tying a necktie.
- Pom-pom scarf:
  - Supplies:
    - » 2-inch pom-poms
    - » Needles
    - » Embroidery floss
  - Instructions:
    This project couldn't be simpler. Just string the pom-poms with the needle and floss and secure at both ends. If the time runs out before teens get the scarf made, provide bags and let them take home pom-poms to finish the project at home.
- Fleece scarf:
  - Supplies:
    - » Fleece in multiple colors (make sure some of the colors are suitable for the guys)
    - » Scissors and/or a rotary cutter
    - » Straight edge
  - Instructions:
    - » Cut the fleece into 8-inch strips.
    - » At the bottom of the strip, cut fringe 5 inches in length and with a ½ inch space.

PASSIVE PROGRAM

The Giving Tree Contest

<u>About the program</u>:

This program is somewhat like the Swap programs mentioned in the Introduction and like other programs in which teens bring in something to trade. It can be done for a specified length of time with participants coming in individually, or it can be planned for a single morning.

<u>Suggested number of participants</u>: Unlimited

<u>Suggested program length</u>: 1–2 weeks to trade or get supplies to build a piece of jewelry, and 1 week to display creations.

<u>Publicity</u>: As a passive program, use the Giving Tree in conjunction with a jewelry-inspired book display.

<u>Evaluation</u>: To track the number of teens who participate in the Giving Tree during the two-week period either to contribute jewelry or to trade jewelry, have them complete a sign-in form or pick up a ticket at a predetermined desk in the library. They will deposit these tickets in a sealed container next to the tree. The tickets can be removed daily or at the end of the program. This is an easy way to get statistics for the extended program.

For the single day program, ask participants as they are leaving if they have enjoyed the opportunity to make, trade, or decorate a piece of jewelry.

<u>Before the program date</u>:

Start off by collecting unwanted pieces of costume jewelry from the staff or buying inexpensive pieces at a local secondhand shop. They may even donate a few items if they are overstocked. You may also go to a craft shop and purchase inexpensive items to decorate jewelry or beads and string for them to create a piece of jewelry.

Prepare a sign-in form or have another staff member there to ask teens to show their library card. It will be a good time to have them get a library card if they do not have one. This will give you an opportunity to find out if they are planning to donate, trade, or create a piece of jewelry. This will help you locate the participants who may not have a piece of jewelry to swap.

<u>Day of the program</u>:

Place a jewelry tree in the Teen area and invite teens to bring outdated or unwanted jewelry to hang on the tree. You can decide to have them pick an item from the tree for each item they donate or allow them to select an item. If space is available, have supplies on hand for teens to spruce up the items they chose or make "new" jewelry out of them. You will need very small sacks for participants to use to take home their pieces of jewelry. Have participants who do not have a library card complete an application and sign in for a ticket to select a piece of jewelry.

When the program begins, allow participants to go to the jewelry tree and trade a piece of jewelry, or to collect a piece of jewelry from the tree, or go to the craft area to select items to build a piece of jewelry. If you have participants who do not have jewelry to swap or do not wish to choose a piece of jewelry from the tree, make sure you have supplies for them to take home to create a necklace or bracelet.

Ask participants to bring back any jewelry they create or change the design of at the end of the program for a display in the library. You might even choose to award a blue ribbon to the best designed or re-created piece of jewelry, a red ribbon for the runner-up, and white ribbons for others who have done a good job.

BIBLIOGRAPHY

Fiction

Jewels of Sofia Tate by Doris Etiennem, Dundurn, 2009
Prophecy of the Gems by Flavia Bujor, HarperCollins Children's Books, 2005

Nonfiction

Beadalicious: 25 fresh, Unforgettable Jewelry Projects for Beads Old and New by Sonya Nimri, Potter Craft, 2008

Bead Simple: Essential Techniques for Making Jewelry Just the Way You Want It by Susan Beal, Tauton Press, 2008

Button It Up: 80 Amazing Vintage Button Projects for Necklaces, Bracelets, Embellishments, House wares & More by Susan Beal, Tauton Press, 2009

Cool Jewels: Beading Projects for Teens by Naomi Fujrnoto, Kalmbach, 2007

D.I.Y. Girl: Do It Yourself: The Real Girl's Guide to Making Everything from Lip Gloss to Lamps by Jennifer Bonnell, Puffin, 2003

Duct Tape Bags, Instructables.com, 2011

The Earring Style Book: Making Designer Earrings, Capturing Celebrity Style, and Getting the Look for Less by Stephanie A. Wells, Potter Craft, 2010

Gemstones by Emma Fox. DK Publishing, 1994

Gemstones by Emma Fox, DK Publishing, 1997

The Girl's World Book of Jewelry: 50 Cool Design to Make by Rain Newcomb, Lark Books, 2004.

Handmade Underground Jewelry: 25 Fun Projects for All Occasions by Shannon LeVart, Wiley, 2009

The Hip Handbag Book by Sherri Haab, Watson-Guptish, 2004

Jewels: A Secret History by Victoria Finlay, Random House Trade Paperback, 2007

Junk Jewelry: 25 Extraordinary Designs to Create from Ordinary Objects by Jane Eldershaw, Potter Craft, 2008

Junk to Jewelry by Brenda Schweder, Kalmbach Books, 2007

The Naughty Secretary Club: The Working Girl's Guide to Handmade Jewelry by Jennifer Perkins, North Light Books, 2008

Refashion Bags: Upcycle Anything into High Style Handbags by Faith Kilkeney, Potter Craft, 2009

7,000 Years of Jewelry by Hugh Tait, Firefly Books, 2007

Sew What! Bags: 18 Pattern-Free Projects You Can Customize to Fit Your Needs by Lexie Barnes, Storey Publishing, LLC, 2009

Simply Gemstones by Nancy Alden, Potter Craft, 2009

Steampunk Style Jewelry, Victorian, Fantasy and Mechanical Necklaces, Bracelets and Earrings by Jen Campbell, Creative Publishing International, 2010

Resource for Librarians

Shrink Art Jewelry by Karen Phillips, Klutz, 2007 (This book is spiral bound, so it is better as a resource book.)

Websites

The web is an excellent place to find ideas, instructions, and what other libraries are doing.

I spy dyi @ http://ispy-diy.blogspot.com/

For jewelry making, check out Winnipeg Public Library Teen Programs in a Box

5

SHHH! Shoes, Hats, and Hair Accessories Happenings

This chapter covers **SHHH—S**hoes, **H**ats and **H**air **H**appenings, and many of the programs will require the purchase of more expensive items unless the teens understand they must provide them. While they might be able to make off with a sibling's worn-out pair of sneakers for the Rotten Sneaker contest, they will need to bring in a pair of their own sneakers if they want to decorate a pair of sneakers to wear.

SHOES

Shoes not only protect our feet, but they also enhance our outfits. The styles of shoes have changed over time. Until the mass production of shoes, many people couldn't afford them. With mass production, shoes became more affordable. Going barefoot often symbolizes poverty. Today most women and many men have multiple pairs of shoes. Shoes are versatile; different shoes have different purposes.

ACTIVE PROGRAMS

Sneaky Sneakers (Transform Your Sneakers)

About the program:

Everyone wears sneakers, but there are sneakers and then there are sneakers. Custom footwear is in vogue, so why not customize your sneakers?

Suggested number of participants: 1–25

Suggested program length: 1½–2 hours

Publicity: The Sneaky Sneakers flyer should have an easily seen statement about bringing a pair of canvas sneakers, preferably white, to transform and some note about what those who do not bring shoes should bring instead. Since participants need to bring shoes, you might want to have a registration process where those taking the reservations ask if the teens will have a pair of shoes with them.

<u>Before the program date</u>:

- Gather supplies:
  - Fabric paint
  - Fabric markers
  - Outdoor Mod Podge
  - Pony beads
  - Old newspapers and teen magazines
  - Tissue paper
  - Foam brushes and scissors
  - Printouts of sneakers for teens who forget to bring sneakers
  - Colored markers and colored pencils for teens who have forgotten to bring sneakers to design a sneaker
  - Brown bags to use as a base to dry sneakers

<u>Day of the program</u>:

Before beginning the craft project, provide the teens with verbal instructions about the craft supplies (as listed above) they will be using to transform their sneakers and encourage them to be as creative as they want.

<u>Instructions</u>:

- Choose your colors of tissue paper or cut out pictures from magazines.
- When you have your tissue paper torn and picture found, decide how you want to arrange your design.
- Use fabric markers to write words or a message.
- Begin at the toe along the sole, brush on the decoupage solution.
- Lay tissue pieces or pictures. Overlapping edges creates an interesting design.
- Brush on a top coat of outdoor decoupage solution.
- Continue until the design is complete. Let dry thoroughly. Multiple coats will give you better protection.
- String beads or paint a design on the laces for a complete design.
- Have a brown bag to set the shoes on and to transport them home.

Paint Ceramic Shoes

<u>About the program</u>:

All programs need not be elaborate affairs. At times a simple, easy program is what is needed. Paint Ceramic Shoes can also be used as an activity at other, shorter shoe programs, or you can add this activity at a Teens Advisory meeting by having teens paint ceramic shoes or other pieces during the meeting. Guys may prefer to paint skateboards, guitars, or other pieces that are available. This program would be good for libraries with limited space and staff.

<u>Publicity</u>: Because this program has a cost involved, you may wish to have teens preregister so that you can offer them the opportunity to attend.

<u>Before the program date</u>:

- Gather supplies:
  - Ceramic shoes can be purchased at the Ceramic Superstore (www.Ceramicsuper store.com) for about $6.00 to $12.00 each; several varieties are available, including a high-heeled shoe (designed to be a cell phone holder), a flip flop (designed to be a box), and a fashion boot (designed to be a vase).
  - Acrylic paint, including some glitter paint for a little glam
  - Brushes
  - Spray on clear glaze
  - Paper plates, to put paint on
  - Paper towels for cleaning brushes
  - Refreshments, if you are planning to have refreshments

<u>Instructions</u>:

- Choose a shoe or other object.
- Decide on the paint scheme and paint—the paint dries fast.
- If a color doesn't work, just paint over the offending color.
- When the shoe is painted, spray the shoe with a clear glaze. This is best done outside.
- While the pieces dry, have refreshments.

All about Shoes

<u>About the program</u>:

All about Shoes is a combination of activities about shoes. Some of the activities could be programs by themselves, such as the Paint Ceramic Shoes described above. Other activities could be added to other programs, or this can be a program in and of itself. When this is a stand-alone program, you must be mindful, in choosing your activities, to describe in the publicity which items participants need to bring.

<u>Suggested number of participants</u>: Unlimited, or while there are supplies

<u>Suggested program length</u>: 1 to 1½ hours

<u>Publicity</u>: If you are going to have participants Walk the Walk, you must put in your publicity that girls should bring a pair of high-heeled shoes and boys should bring a pair of dress shoes to wear. If you are willing to provide shoes, you might want to suggest that they bring something to cover their feet in these "mystery" shoes. This will cover the situations where participants do not bring shoes and will be wearing shoes you have selected at a local secondhand store.

<u>Supplies</u>: high-heeled shoes and men's dress shoes from a secondhand store and chocolate gold coins if you are planning to have the "Walk the Walk" activity

<u>Before the program date</u>:

Select a speaker who will present a program on choosing shoes for different activities. If at all possible, have the speaker bring some examples of different types of shoes for different occasions. See "Introduction" for more information on hosting a speaker.

Decide what activities will be part of the program. Below are just some ideas for an All about Shoes program. You can mix and match to fit your teens' preferences.

Icebreakers:

- As teens assemble, have trivia questions available for them to work on separately or ask other teens for answers. See Appendix L, "Shoes throughout History Trivia Quiz," for more information.
  - Cinderella and the Prince is a good icebreaker for any shoe party. As guests arrive, ask them to remove their shoes and put them in the front of the program area.
    - » When all teens have arrived, ask them to pick out one shoe that doesn't belong to them.
    - » Have them mingle and get to know each other while trying to find the owner of the shoe they have chosen.
    - » The first boy to find the owner of the girl's shoe he selected is the Prince, and the girl becomes Cinderella.
    - » Keep mingling until all shoes have their correct owners.
    - » Have a small prize for the first Prince and Cinderella. Don't forget to buy a gift for the Prince and Cinderella if you choose this icebreaker.
- Walk the Walk:

  Teens are just beginning to wear high heels, and walking in them is different and difficult. If this activity is part of your larger program, ask teens to bring in a pair of heels. Have several pairs of heels available for the teens who forget. Get various heights and sizes. Teenage guys might want to try this for fun.

Instructions:

- Ask everyone to put on their shoes and try walking in them.
- When they have walked around the room for a minute or two, have them stop, sit down, and talk about walking in heels.
- Demonstrate the proper way to walk in heels. Show one of the YouTube videos listed below to see the proper way to walk.
- Try walking in heels again, pause, and discuss the difference.
- Now, just for fun, have a relay race. Divide the teens into teams and see which team can complete the walk first, without losing their balance or stumbling. To make it more difficult, have them place a book on their head and walk. Have chocolate gold coins for a reward.
- Website: http://shoes.about.com/od/fashionfootwear/ht/walk_high_heels.htm
- YouTube: How to Walk in Stilettos and How to Walk in High Heels with Catwalk Confidence

Day of the program:

Set up your room with chairs in rows for participants to listen to the speaker.

Place your boxes of shoes on one side of the room. After participants have heard the speaker, they should help move the chairs from rows out of the center of the room to allow space to practice walking in shoes.

PASSIVE PROGRAM

Rotten Sneaker Contest

<u>About the program</u>:

A Rotten Sneaker Contest asks teens to bring in their grungiest, smelliest, dirtiest, ugliest worn sneakers. The sneakers will be put on display until the judges selected to judge vote on the most offensive sneaker. The Rotten Sneaker Contest is a perfect way to advertise the Sneaky Sneaker program. If the contest is an advertisement for the Sneaky Sneaker program, present the winners at the program. See the Introduction for more information on Formal Exhibits.

<u>Suggested number of participants</u>: Unlimited

<u>Suggested program length</u>: 2–4 weeks

<u>Publicity</u>: Publicize the contest by posting a call for entries of Rotten Sneakers on your library's website, Facebook page, and young adult areas. Be sure to highlight the day or days sneakers may be submitted at the library and the day the winner will be named.

<u>Before the program date</u>:

- Choose your judges. Have at least three judges, the owner of a shoe store or sports store that sells sneakers, a staff member, a podiatrist, a teacher, or a teen who hasn't entered the contest. If you have someone as judge who sells sneakers, this person could be asked to donate a pair of sneakers to the winner(s) (who will obviously need a new pair of sneakers). The store or stores may be willing to display the winners in the store.
- Other prizes can be smaller, such as a can of Febreze or Dr. Scholl's Odor X, a small trophy, or some other gift.
- Prepare your registration form.
- Get a marking pen to mark the bottom of the sneakers, and decide what to use for numbers to put beside the sneakers on display.

<u>Day of the program</u>:

When the sneakers come into the library, register the sneaker by getting the owner's name, phone number, and email address.

- Each sneaker gets a number which will be put on the bottom of the sneaker and next to the sneaker when it goes on display.

<u>After the program beginning date</u>:

A day or two after the deadline for submission the sneakers will be judged.
Judging the Contest:

- Have judges vote for the sneaker they believe is the grungiest, dirtiest, smelliest, most offensive sneaker in the bunch. You may choose to have them award a second and a third prize.
- Winner(s) will be notified by email or phone. Take photos of the winners with their sneakers. Post the pictures on the library's Internet sites.

Decorative Sneaker Exhibit

About the program:

Teens decorate sneakers at home and bring them to the library to be put on display. An exhibit can easily be turned into a contest by inviting three people to judge the creations. The winner is given a gift certificate for a pair of sneakers. If a local store is willing to donate a gift certificate for a pair of sneakers, ask if it will display the winner's shoes at the store for a week. See the Introduction for more information on Formal Exhibits.

Before the program date:

- Create a list of supplies teens will need to decorate their sneakers at home, including the following (which is similar to the list of supplies in your active program above):
  ◦ Fabric paint
  ◦ Fabric markers
  ◦ Outdoor Mod Podge
  ◦ Pony beads

If the budget allows, provide them with a few of the supplies. Put some supplies in a bag and check out the supplies to the teens.

Custom Sneaker Art Exhibit

About the program:

Teens are invited to create a new sneaker. This differs from the Design a Sneaker program in that the teen is creating a new sneaker using a paper template. Participating teens will be given a paper template of a sneaker or they can create their own sneaker. All the designs will be exhibited in the library. See the "Introduction" for more information on Formal Exhibits.

Before the program date:

- Set some criteria for the artwork. For example: it must be original, and it should have "acceptable" graphics and words. Specify the type of media that can be used (paint, colored pencils, or markers). Other criteria can be added.
- Decide how the artwork will be displayed.
- Select a date for all designs to be returned to the library; two to four weeks would be ideal.
- One source for sneaker patterns is *The Sneaker Coloring Book* (Laurence King Publishers, 2010), or check out the Internet.
- Enlarge the patterns to 8x11 and print on card stock.
- Have teens pick up the patterns at the designated desk.

Day of the program:

- Create the display:
  ◦ One idea is to hang twine or small rope on a wall or around the teen room or area, and then hang the artwork by clothespins that have been spray painted.

HATS

The main purpose of a hat is protection. Like shoes, hats have changed purpose and style over time. Throughout history hats become popular, and then they fall out of fashion. Some celebrities have become famous for their hats. The Queen of England is always seen in public in a hat. Two famous horse races, the Royal Ascot and the Kentucky Derby, are known for the large, flamboyant hats worn by the ladies. When you think of President Lincoln, you think of his tall stovepipe hat, and First Lady Jackie Kennedy was known for her pillbox hats. Some cultures are known for a particular head covering. Teens often wear hats, usually more casual ones, such as the baseball cap, often reversed with the bill on the back of the neck. Teens will often wear a hat to make a statement or to stand out from the crowd. Pop culture idols will often influence the hats that teens wear.

ACTIVE PROGRAMS

Favorite Book Hat Contest

About the program:

The purpose of the Favorite Book Hat Contest is to create a hat that tells or depicts the story of a favorite book. Anything that can be attached to a hat may be used. This can also be a passive program. For refreshments, consider having a Mad Hatter Tea (see next program for more information) to tie in with the program.

Suggested number of participants: 10–25

Suggested length of time: 1½–2 hours

Before the program date:

- If you are planning to start with the Bingo game found in Appendix M, you will need to create more Bingo cards for the participants to use, so review the instructions carefully and make your preparations.
- Gather supplies:
  ○ Plain hats—some styles of hats would work better than others, for example, stove pip hats (these are usually striped, but that might make the design more interesting), neon fedoras, and black top hats. Oriental Trading Company is one source for hats, and there are sure to be others. Just be sure the hats are of fabric so it will be easier to attach the decorations.
  ○ Material and trim
  ○ Paper, to cut out designs
  ○ Staplers and staples
  ○ Hot glue stick and glue gun
  ○ Cups and saucers or glasses, depending upon the beverage chosen for the Mad Hatter Tea
  ○ Food for the tea

Day of the program:

- A game of Bingo in Appendix M could start the session, seat the students, and prepare the participants for the remainder of the program.

- Trivia games can be icebreakers as teens arrive. They can walk around and get help with the trivia question from other teens. See Appendix N "Famous Hats"; or Appendix O "Hats, Hats, and More Hats Quiz Reference Scavenger Game."
- Play a number game. See Appendix P "Famous Hat People" for more information.
- Creating their Favorite Book Hat:
  - Let the teens select the hat they'd like to decorate.
  - If needed, provide an example of how to use the materials. Give them plenty of time to experiment and create with new designs on their hats.

Mad Hatter Tea

This program can be a stand-alone, which allows participants to learn a little about proper behavior at a more formal event without making an issue of proper behavior at such an event.

About the program:

As a stand-alone program, participants may want to bring the hats they created at the Favorite Book Hat Contest, or they may prefer to bring another hat to wear for the tea.

Suggested number of participants: 10–25

Suggested program length: 1½–2 hours

Publicity: Because of the limited number of participants, you may wish to limit your audience. Therefore, publicity in the teen area or the library may be sufficient.

Before the program:

If you do not wish to demonstrate how to set a tea service and proper behavior at a tea party, you may see if one of your colleagues in the library is willing to do this. This might be a good opportunity to engage the school librarian in the program and invite the person teaching this at the school.

Before the program date:

Make sure you have the appropriate table coverings and table settings as well as dishes for displaying the refreshments. While paper plates and napkins can do, if that is all that is available, tea rooms and hotels serving tea do not use paper or plastic, and you want to be as close to reality as you can be with this one.

You might want to see if you can find some hats for participants who do not bring a hat to the tea.

Day of the program date:

Have tables covered with tablecloths, preferably nice white ones and napkins: One table will be for the refreshments, and the other table(s) will be for sitting and having tea.

- On the refreshment table:
  - Arrange tea sandwiches on tiered serving dishes if you have them. If these are not available, have nice dishes.
  - Small muffins or scones
  - Small desserts, cookies, brownies, truffles

- ◦ At one end of the table have a silver tea service, if possible. Or you can serve lemonade from glass pitchers.
- • Participants will observe the demonstration, and then they will sit down for their tea.

As participants arrive, if they do not have a hat, you may wish to let them select one to wear.

<u>After the Program</u>: Perhaps members of your Advisory Committee can help with the cleanup.

Hat Program as Knitting Program

Hats are a good starting project for libraries that have knitting programs or are thinking of one. If your library has or would like to have an altruistic program knitting hats for homeless children or caps for newborn babies, this would be a good opportunity for teens to get involved and give back to their community.

<u>Suggested number of participants</u>: 10+, depending upon how many volunteer instructors

<u>Suggested program length</u>: 2–6 weeks, with weekly meetings until interest wanes

<u>Publicity</u>: Ask participants to purchase knitting needles and one skein of yarn unless your budget permits your purchasing these. This is a program that you might engage a women's service organization to donate supplies and instructors. You may want to ask for preregistration to determine the numbers who might attend.

<u>Before the program date</u>:

- • Arrange for volunteer instructors. If you go to a service group to ask for volunteer instructors, remind them they will be working with teens.
- • If you are furnishing yarn and knitting needles, purchase those.
- • Get refreshments. For this group, you will need to thank the volunteers and encourage the participants to return for another session.

<u>Day of the program</u>:

- • Arrange the room so that volunteers can both demonstrate how to knit, as well as move around easily to help the teens and to answer questions.

Decorate Your Hair

<u>About the program</u>:
Like hats, hair accessories come and go as fashion accessories. Pop culture creates the interest in adding accessories to the hair, and headbands and other hair accessories are making a comeback. Hair accessories are easy and fun to make. They are just right for a teen library program.

<u>Suggested number of participants</u>: 10–25

<u>Suggested program length</u>: 1 to 1½ hours

<u>Before the program date</u>:

- • Gather supplies
  - ◦ ½ to 1 yard per project, depending on the width of the wire ribbon (depending on how large and tight you want your flowers)

- ○ Coordinating strong thread
- ○ Needle
- ○ Hair clip or headband
- ○ Hot glue gun and glue sticks

<u>Day of the program:</u>

- Icebreakers
  As teens assemble, have trivia questions available for them to work on separately or ask other teens for answers.

See Appendix Q "Name that Hairstyle" and Appendix R "Hair through History Trivia" for more information.

- Ribbon Flower Barrett/Headband

<u>Instructions:</u>

- Pull on the wire of one side of the ribbon to ruffle. Ruffle the entire length of your piece of ribbon. Not all wire ribbon is the same. Some are more fragile, so pull gently. Leave a few inches of wire hanging out of the ends, but clip away the rest to get it out of your way.
- To start, fold your ribbon back and forth a few times (on the side of ribbon that you just pull the wire). Using quilting thread, run a stitch through the ribbon several times to secure.
- Start wrapping the ribbon around. Secure each wrap by stitching all the way through the layers in a star pattern.
- Once it is large enough to be difficult to stitch through all the layers, secure by stitching to the previous layer.
- When you come to the end of the ribbon, fold the corner of ribbon back inside to hide the raw edge. Stitch in place. Cut off excess wire.
- Attach to a hair clip or headband using a hot glue gun.

For variations:

- Attach pin to make pin corsage to accessorize clothing or hats.
- Add a few feathers to each side of the flower.
- Glue rhinestones to a few of the petals.
- Another fun idea would be to make a headband from old ties. The instructions can be found in *The Naughty Secretary Club: The Working Girl's Guide to Handmade Jewelry* by Jennifer Perkins, page 59 (North Light Books, 2008).

Shh!

<u>About the program:</u>

A library is a great place to have a Shh! program. That doesn't mean it's going to be quiet. Shh! is a program combining activities from the programs on shoes, hats, and hair accessories. Select activities that you didn't get to use in a program. Or mix it up, using a couple of favorites and some new activities. Review other programs for activities that will work with the Shh! theme.

<u>Suggested number of participants</u>: 10–25+, depending on activities

<u>Suggested program length</u>: 1–1½ hours

<u>Day of the program</u>:

- Numbered Chair Game
- Select questions from the trivia questions about shoes and hats.

See Appendix L "Shoes through Court History Trivia Quiz" or Appendix P "Famous Hat People" for more information.

- Shh! Bingo
- Using the blank Bingo cards in the appendix, use styles of shoes and hats and the names of hair accessories for your Bingo words.
- For prizes, have hats, inexpensive flip flops, slipper socks, or hair accessories for teens to choose from.
- Other Crafts:
  - Painted ceramic shoes
  - Make a headband; have some leather cording to braid for the guys.
  - Use the Sneaky Sneakers instructions to decorate a sneaker.
  - Host a Mad Hatter Tea (see above for ideas for a Mad Hatter Tea).

BIBLIOGRAPHY

Fiction

Because of Anya by Margaret Peterson Haddix, Simon & Schuster Children's Publishing, 2004
Bella in the Slouch Hat by Mim Mathis, Phoenix International, 2010
Best Foot Forward by Joan Bauer, Speak, 2006
Cindy Ella by Robin Palmer, Speak, 2008
Dancing in Red Shoes Will Kill You by Dorine Corroine, HarperTeen, 2005
Golden: A Retelling of Rapunzel by Cameron Doky, Simon Pulse, 2007
Princess of Glass by Jessica Day George, Bloomsbury USA, 2010
Rules of the Road by Joan Bauer, Speak, 2005
Sirenz by Charlotte Bennardo, Flux, 2011
Standing for Socks by Elissa Weissman, Simon and Schuster Children's, 2010
Why I Let My Hair Grow Out by Maryrose Wood, Berkley Trade, 2007
Withering Tights (Misadventures of Tallulah Casey) by Louise Rennison, HarperTeen, 2011

Nonfiction

Altered Shoes: A Step-By-Step Guide to Making Your Footwear Fabulous by Marty Stevens-Heebner, KP Books, 2009
Art & Sole: Contemporary Sneakers & Design by Intercity, Laurence King Publisher, 2008
Custom Kicks: Personalized Footwear by Kim Smits, Laurence King Publishers, 2008
Dangles and Bangles: 25 Funky Accessories to Make and Wear by Sherri Haab, Watson-Guptill, 2005
Fashion Geek: Clothes Accessories by Diana Eng, North Light Books, 2009

If the Shoe Fits: Voices from Cinderella by Laura Whipple, Simon and Schuster Children's Books, 2002

Socks Appeal: 16 Fun & Funky Friends Sewn from Socks by Brenna Maloney, C & T Publishing, 2010

Stupid Sock Creatures, Making Quirky, Lovable Figures from Cast-Off Socks by John Murphy, Lark Books, Sterling Publishing Co. Inc., 2005

Vans: Off the Wall: Stories of Sole from Vans Originals by Doug Palladini Abrams, 2009.

Resources for Librarians

Custom Kicks by Kim Smits, Laurence King Publishing, 2008

Sneaker Coloring Book by Daniel Jarosch and Henrik Klingel, Laurence King Publishing, 2010

DVD

Just for Kicks, produced by Grandmaster Caz

6

For Guys Only or Guy Style

For every teenage boy there is a time when he must venture into the world of the unknown and start clothes shopping for himself. The words "fashion" and "teenage boy" don't exactly go together like bread and butter, but with a little help, anything is possible. Teenage guys are either interested in what they wear, or they put on the first thing that catches their eye and it doesn't matter what it looks like. However, guys are interested in catching the eyes of girls, and in order to make a good impression, many begin to care about what they put on and how they look.

According to men's fashion expert Andy Gilchrist, "Researchers have come up with some scientific evidence to support the fact that what you wear really does make a difference in how you influence the world around you." He says that looking good may even affect your grades (fashion.about.com/cs/...bigguystyle.htm).

Middle school guys who are just starting to shop for themselves may be intimidated by the process. This is a good time to get them involved in selecting clothes for themselves. Don't let moms attend; guys need to feel comfortable talking about this subject. Use this chapter to create partnerships with organizations like the Boy Scouts or other groups that have a large number of 'tween and teen boys.

PROGRAMS

Looking Good

About the program:

This program is offered as a slow approach rather than a one-time event. You need to move cautiously, getting and keeping a teen's attention with no abrupt movements, or they will scatter like sheep. Without a sheep dog to corral them, it will be difficult to get them back.

Suggested number of participants: unlimited

Suggested program length: over 2 to 3 weeks, or until interest wanes

Publicity: Guys might be reluctant to attend a program about what to wear, so start with handouts in the teen area that they can slip into their backpacks and read when no one is watching them.

Before the program date:

- Print out tips on what to wear and a list of Websites. Make them attractive and short, and include pictures. One handout in this book is Appendix S "Glossary of Guy

Styles." You may wish to add to this, depending upon your own audience. While it is unlikely at this time that your audience might not understand when someone says you should wear khakis, you need to make sure your guys can see what khakis are. If they have something to refer to, they don't have to ask and thus appear dumb.

- Other handouts might include Appendix T "Hygiene High Jinks"; Appendix U "Looking and Smelling Good"; and Appendix V "Tips for the Well-Groomed Guy."
- Set up an inspiration board in the teen area.
  - You will be featuring pictures of guys who are dressed well and other pictures of guys who don't quite get it. Girls might get involved in this part of the program. The first time you have this program, you can look in magazines for pictures. You might even check the comics for the "don't get it" figures in strips such as "Zits." If you are going to repeat this, you might ask for some of your teens to create these looks, and then they can post them on the inspiration board.
- Divide the inspiration board into two halves. One is "The Right Look" and the other is "Fashion Disasters."
- Provide a basket of old magazines or department store ads and scissors.
- Below the signs, write the instructions:
  - Cut out pictures of guys who have the right look, and place them under "The Right Look" area. Take a piece of paper and write in ten words or less why this is "the right look."
  - If you find a picture of a guy who doesn't have the right look, cut it out and put it on the "Fashion Disasters" side. Take a piece of paper and write in ten words or less why this is a "fashion disaster" look.

Luke's (or whatever you choose to call him) New Look: Two Basics, Many Styles

About the program:

The purpose of this program is to show guys that you can take two basic items of clothing, a pair of jeans and a T-shirt, and make many different outfits by adding accessories, different shoes, and a shirt, jacket, or sweater.

Suggested number of participants: Unlimited

Suggested program length: The length of time you want to have the mannequin out will depend on the participation of the teens. If the teens in your library don't show an interest in changing Luke's style, you may want to have him visit only one week. If there is real interest in the program, then leave it up until the interest begins to wane.

Before the program date:

- Put a male mannequin in the Teen area dressed in a simple T-shirt and jeans, with a pair of sneakers sitting on the floor.
- Gather teen clothing from staff, secondhand stores, church bazaars, and garage sales. You may be donating the leftover items back to the secondhand store when the program is over.

- On a closet rack or pipe clothes hanger (see Appendix F), have other shirts, sweaters, and different types of T-shirts.
- In a basket have the accessories, to show what adding a little extra can do for the overall look.
- On a wall or on a closet rack, put a sign with the instructions:
  - Give the mannequin the name Luke, or another name of your choice. You might ask your Teen Advisory committee to name him, and try to make sure the name is not a current teen they know because that could be considered "bullying."
  - On the sign say: Luke needs a new look. Change Luke's (or whatever you choose to name him) basic look by adding a different T-shirt, or adding a shirt to the basic "T." Use anything on the rack or in the basket. See how many different looks you can give Luke.
- Plan to keep a camera handy to take pictures of Luke's new looks to add to your Website and other social networking sites. These pictures can also be used in another program.

Shopping Paralysis

About the program:

Do your teens dread or hate the thought of buying something new? Do you know if they go into a store and grab the first thing that they see so they can get out of the store? Do you think they may have "shopping paralysis"?

You are going to offer shopping intervention. Shopping Paralysis will provide you with the tools to help teens learn how to walk into a store with confidence. When they walk out, they will be proud of what they have purchased. At the end of your program, your teens will be on their way to ending Shopping Paralysis.

Suggested number of participants: 10–25

Suggested program length: 1–1½ hours

Publicity: Your flyers will reflect the program and the guest speakers, if you have guest speakers. You should credit a shop owner if clothing is going to be shown from the store.

Before the program date:

- See Introduction for planning guest speakers programs.
- Talk to a local clothing store or stores where teen guys shop and ask if someone from the store would be on a panel to give advice to teenage guys about how to dress, what to look for, and how to put together outfits. As you will have read in the Introduction, when approaching the store, be prepared. Provide them with the suggested day and time of the program, what you'd like for them to do, and the amount of compensation, if they desire it. If you would like them to bring clothing to show how to mix and match, explain this and ask if that is a possibility.
- Select persons who may be fashion experts for a panel discussion. If it is a panel discussion, you should have two or more speakers or one speaker with a PowerPoint.

- The speaker or panel should be no more than 30 to 45 minutes.
- Plan to be the speaker yourself. You can use the pictures from the two programs above to create a PowerPoint presentation or create your own, using men's fashion do's and don'ts.
- If speakers are bringing clothing, you will need a garment rack or a pipe clothes hanger (see Appendix F) and a couple of mannequins.
- Boys love to eat, and teens eat a great deal, so you will need more snacks than you might imagine.
- Gather materials for a follow-up activity, choosing from those mentioned below.

Day of the program:

- If the speakers bring clothes with them, help them hang the clothes with wooden or plastic hangers. Let your speakers know what you will have for them to use. They might even bring or donate a mannequin if you have a place to store it.
- Check all the electronics that will be used to see that they are working.
- Introduce the speaker or the panel for their discussion or PowerPoint presentation. If you find the audience is drifting off, you should interrupt with a question and then ask if others in the audience have questions. This will allow them to wrap up after they have answered any other questions. Be sure to inform the speakers that you might be doing this. It should help them be aware of their audience, especially if they have not presented to 'tweens and teens in the past.
- Move to close the program with refreshments, or if teens still seem to need an activity, choose from those below.

Shopping Journal

These can be composition books from an office supply story (about $1 each).

Supplies:

- Pens
- Old magazines; any teen magazine will work, including skateboarding and music magazines, catalogs, and advertisements
- Scissors
- Glue

Instructions:

- Go through the magazines, catalogs, and ads for clothes the guys think they like.
- After cutting those out, they can make inspirations pages or a wish list with pictures. The inspiration pages and wish list can help them when they go shopping.

Duct Tape Wallets

<u>Supplies</u>:

- Duct tape is now available in many colors, patterns, and even sheets
- Scissors
- Template of a dollar bill

<u>Instructions</u>:

Remember to create one or more of these before you demonstrate how to do it to the group.

- If using rolls of duct tape, make overlapping strips of duct tape a little larger than a dollar bill. Overlap at least ½ inch. Note: Making duct tape sheets is the first step in almost any duct tape construction project.
- If using sheets of duct tape, you can skip the first step.
- Trim the overlapping pieces a bit larger than a dollar bill.
- Flip the first strips over and tape on the flip side. Make your strips overlapping the edges by at least ½ inch.
- Flip it over again and trim the corners at 45 degree angles. Then fold the tape to make sealed edges.
- Make another sheet that is a bit smaller than the first sheet (but still larger than the dollar bill). Seal the top edge, but use the other edges to fashion the sheets to make a pocket.
- If you are using sheets, you will just need to use a second sheet to make a pocket.
- Using sheets is easier, but using strips allows you to customize your sheet by using different colors and patterns of tape (see www.octanecreative.com/ducttape/howto/).

My Skin and Me

For this program the Appendixes listed earlier in this chapter, "Glossary of Guy Styles," "Looking and Smelling Good," and "Tips for the Well-Groomed Guy" will provide additional information.

<u>About the program</u>:

The early teen years are when both young men and women experience many physical changes. They are faced with problems with acne on their skin, which becomes very noticeable on their faces. Hopefully they not only think more about body odor and other general hygiene problems, but they are interested in correcting any issues. Many have parents or older siblings to talk to them and assist them. Others may not be so lucky. The library is a safe environment to help them understand what is happening.

<u>Suggested number of participants</u>: 10–25

<u>Suggested program length</u>: 1–1½ hours

<u>Before the program date</u>:

- Find a skin care professional who can talk to guys about what is happening to their bodies. Ask this professional if it is possible to provide some samples of skin care products, or check out department stores or other beauty/skin care businesses for these products for men. If possible, have a male do the presentation. See the "Introduction" for more information on Finding Guest Speakers.

- Make up some cool gift bags with some sample products. Small drawstring bags would be a nice touch.
- Refreshments

Day of the program:

- Have the speaker talk for about 30 minutes. Provide the speaker with enough time to talk one-on-one with the guys after the presentation. Boys may be shy about asking questions, so the speaker will need to be proactive.
- Make this an interactive program, letting them experiment with different products (30 minutes). For example, have the speaker demonstrate the proper way to wash your face and let the guys practice.
- Provide refreshments as interest begins to wane.
- As they leave, give them their gift bags.

Recommended websites:

www.myjellybean.com
www.mookychick.co.uk/style
www.coolmenhair.com
www.wikihow.com/Category:Grooming-for-Boys

This site has several articles for teenage guys on fashion and grooming.

BIBLIOGRAPHY

Nonfiction

Ductigami: The Art of the Tape by Joe Wilson, Boston Mills Press, 2006
Got Tape? by Ellie Schiedermayer, Krausse, 2002
Just Duct Tape It by Leisure Arts, 2011
Kid's Guide to Duct Tape Projects by Sherie Bell-Rehwoldt, Capstone Press, 2001
Stick It!: 99 DIY Duct Tape Projects by T.L. Bonaddio, Running Press Kids, 2007 (This is spiral bound and may be best used as a resource for librarians.)
What's Happening to My Body? Books for Boys by Lynda Madaras, Newmarket Press, 2000

Fiction

Love (and Other Uses for Duct Tape) by Carrie Jones, Flux, 2008

Resource

For Young Men Only by Jeff Felthahn, Multnomah Books, 2008

Mash Up

Combine making duct tape accessories with a program on recycled fashion.

7

Turning Green

Many teens are becoming more conscious of the need to save the environment, to use earth friendly products, and to volunteer for Green organizations. Tap into their passion for this movement by hosting Green programs. Using Green as a theme also presents opportunities to partner with Sustainability Departments and Green organizations. While Green programs may be offered at any time during the year, one should definitely plan for Earth Day. Earth Day helps the entire library focus on good publicity for the community.

PROGRAMS

Green Fashion Show

About the program:

A Green Fashion Show is an informational program for teens to show environmentally friendly fashions and products. The teens get involved by being models as well as attending the program. This program is a good example of a multigenerational program that will entertain and inform all ages. It provides an opportunity to work with the local school librarians because many schools have strong environmental efforts.

A Green Fashion Show may take time to put together. You will need to search out stores that feature green clothing and approach them about working with you as a sponsor of a green fashion show. Don't forget the hair and makeup products for the models. When you have sponsors for the program, you will provide information about their stores to provide teens with shopping information. A Green Fashion Show will take more than your average planning time but could net the library excellent publicity and partnership opportunities. See the "Introduction" for more information on Fashion Shows.

Suggested number of participants: 10–25 for those who want to model in the fashion show, unlimited for an audience

Suggested program length: 1½–2 hours

Publicity: As with other programs involving outside persons, stores, or agencies, publicity for the program must acknowledge their participation. Also, because this has multigenerational appeal and is a hot topic, you may be able to get wider media coverage than for a non-themed style show.

<u>Before the program date</u>:

In addition to the directions, as suggested in Chapter 1 under Fashion Week you will want to have brochures from any agency with environmentally conscious activities. If your city has requirements for separated garbage collection or even for the use of plastic bags in grocery stores, these could be featured on a poster in the room. The focus is on the environment.

ABC, or Trash-to-Treasure Fashion Show

<u>About the program</u>:

Earth Day is a great time to have an ABC (Anything but Clothing) or Trash-to-Treasure Fashion Show. Either of these is not a clothes party but a chance to create an outfit out of recycled material. The first part of the program is to create an outfit from recycled material. The second part of the program is a fashion show during which teens model their creations. This could be done as a single program on Earth Day or as a two-session program culminating on Earth Day. The first week, have the teens create outfits. The second section is the fashion show to highlight their creations.

<u>Suggested number of participants</u>: 10–25

<u>Suggested program length</u>: 2 hours for each of two sessions

<u>Publicity</u>: Have one or more staff members create a wearable item that they have made from recycled material, which they can wear to promote the program. This will put the library staff and patrons into the spirit of the program, help advertise the program, and provide inspiration. If wearing the recycled item is not practical, create an inspiration board with photographs of the items created. You will also want to promote this program by handing out flyers and posting the upcoming event on your Website and Facebook page.

<u>Before the program date</u>:

Start gathering the supplies about a month before the program. Ask staff and library patrons to donate recycled material. Give them a list of items that will be needed.

<u>Supplies</u>:

- Boxes
- Large garbage bags
- Aluminum foil, newspaper
- Tabs from soda pop cans
- Bubble wrap
- Wrapping paper
- Materials to embellish the design, including stickers, jewels, lace, buttons, ribbon, etc.
- A large supply of duct tape; remember that duct tape comes in many different colors and patterns
- Packing tape

- Staples
- String and yarn
- Scissors
- Glue
- Written instructions (see below)
- Refreshments (purchase ahead)

Day of the program:

Instructions:

- Teens can work in teams or individually, depending on the attendance. If the number is sufficient to pair the teens, let them choose their pairs.
- Either hand out the instruction sheet with the supply list, or explain the supplies. Let the teens look over the supplies to get an idea of what they might like to create.
- Encourage them to brainstorm on their possible design; for example, a top, a top and skirt, pants, hat or hair piece, shoes, a purse and jewelry.
- If you decide pairs want to have more than one item, join the pairs into teams of four, six, or eight.
- Use all of the team for ideas, especially if the group seems to be having problems.
- Keep in mind that you have only two hours to create the costume if the program is one session. Finishing touches might be made at the second session when all designs must be modeled.
- When the projects are completed, give each of your pairs or your teams a designer name. Give the outfit a name and write out a description of the outfit. This will go to the Master of Ceremonies to read during the presentation. Don't forget the model's name.
- At the end of the creating two hours in the two-session program, have the team clean up the workspace. Have bins or boxes marked for the different supplies; this will make cleanup go faster, and the staff won't have to sort everything afterwards.
- At the end of the second hour of a four-hour session, have the models ready for the fashion show. While the models get in place, the rest of the team can clean up the workspace.
- Refreshments can be offered during the work session; this will give them energy to keep designing.

Fashion Show:

- Start the music. This is the signal that the fashion show is about to start.
  - At the beginning, remind the audience that applause for the model and creations is appreciated. As the Master of Ceremonies reads the model name, the model walks out and the outfit is described.
  - Have a volunteer or staff member ready to take many photos, just like in all fashion shows. The photos, with parental permission, can later be posted on your library's Website and Facebook page to publicize the event and future teen programs.

<u>After the program</u>:

- The teens can take their outfits home with them. If the outfits were designed by a team, you may wish to keep them in the library. Also, if there are other outfits remaining, display them in the teen area with pictures of the program. Keep some to use for publicity for another recycle program.

FUNcrafts with Recycle Material

<u>About the program</u>:

Another fun title for this program is From Junk to Jewelry. Once a week for a month (four sessions), make fun fashion items from recycled materials. If the thought of one craft program a week for a month is too overwhelming, these projects can be stand-alone programs. Or, consider making it a passive program in which the instructions, a sample, and the supplies are available in the teen area during certain times of the day or week. The teens can also create recycled jewelry at home and bring the pieces into the library for display.

<u>Suggested number of participants</u>: 10–25

<u>Suggested program length</u>: 1–1½ hours

<u>Before the program date</u>:

- While you may locate descriptions of many recycled craft projects, you should use the Teen Advisory Council to brainstorm creative craft ideas. Have them look through books in the collection and decide which projects to highlight.
- When doing recycle programs, you want to start early in gathering the supplies because it may take some time to get everything that will be needed. Look around the library for materials that can be used for the program; for example, old magazines for magazine bracelets, cardboard cores from all of the tape that is used to create bracelets, and old microfiche can be recycled for lots of craft ideas.

<u>Day of the program</u>: Remember, this is held in four sessions over four weeks.

- Week one: paper beads
  ○ Learn to make paper beads from a YouTube video by Threadbanger. The video demonstrates how to make paper beads from old newspapers and from old magazines.
    This video and many other ones, which you can search through for suggestions, are available at http://www.youtube.com/Threadbanger or http://laisdiyprojects.blogspot.com under the title "How to Make Recycled Paper Beads."
- Week two: Bangles and jangles soda pop-can tabs jewelry. For supplies and instructions, use this Website: http://lollyjaneboutique.blogspot.com/2010/05/pop-tab-bracelet-tutorial.html
- Week three: magazine cuff
  <u>Supplies</u>:
  ○ Inner cardboard core from library tape or wooden/plastic bangles
  ○ Magazines

- ○ Decoupage glue
- ○ Foam brushes

Instructions:

- ○ Use paper shredder to cut magazines in long, fine strips. Use a paper cutter if no paper shredder is available.
- ○ Cover section of core or bracelet with decoupage glue, use plenty of decoupage, and lay down magazine strips.
- ○ The strips may be used to create a design by the way they are placed vertically or horizontally. Also, consider using like colors to create a textured look.
- ○ When finished, cover entire cuff with decoupage to seal.

- Week four: puzzle piece jewelry

Supplies:

- ○ Small puzzle pieces
- ○ Jump rings
- ○ Various jewelry findings
- ○ Decoupage glue
- ○ Jewelry pliers
- ○ Awl or dremel

Instructions:

- ○ Several ways can be used to decorate puzzle pieces to make unique pieces.
  - » Glitter them by using ultrafine glitter in your choice of colors. Or, try silver, gold, and bronze for a metallic effect.
  - » Paper them by using tissue paper or pages from magazines and books.
  - » Paint them by using acrylic paints in a variety of colors.
- ○ Pick out several puzzle pieces to decorate. Estimate how many you will need for the type of jewelry you want to create. For example, choose two pieces to create a pair of earrings and maybe seven to nine pieces to create a bracelet.
- ○ Next, decorate by using glitter, paper, or paint. You can choose multiple decorating ideas. Allow time for drying between methods.
- ○ Seal each puzzle piece with decoupage glue.
- ○ Use awl or dremel to drill a hole for jump rings.
- ○ Attach pieces together to create piece desired.

Other projects that may be used for this program are the following:

- Jewelry Holder from old picture frames (see directions in Chapter 4 "Putting on the Bling"). The Abilene Public Library has a great YouTube series, Project Teen, easily found through asking Google to find YouTube Abilene Public Library. It includes Making Charms, Duct Tape Roses, Drawstring T-Shirt Backpacks, and Recycled Credit Card Bracelets. Project 6 is a jewelry organizer made from old picture frames.
- Button Jewelry:

Supplies:

- ○ Buttons
- ○ Beads

- ○ Elastic thread or stretch cord
- ○ Scissors

Instructions:
- ○ Measure the elastic thread or stretch cord by holding it around your wrist, neck, or finger.
- ○ Cut a piece about 6 inches longer than your measurement.
- ○ String on a bead or button and tie to secure about 3 inches from one end.
- ○ Start stringing buttons or beads onto the thread or cord. For the button, string them through the two holes to make the button lay flat, alternate with coordinating beads, if desired. The anchor bead can be removed if desired.

- • Tie Necklace:

Supplies:
- ○ Old ties
- ○ Basic sewing supplies (needle, scissors, thread)
- ○ Chain and jewelry findings (can also use an existing plain necklace with no pendant or other embellishments)
- ○ Optional: additional embellishments
  - » Fancy buttons or pins
  - » Paint fabric /markers
  - » Fabric trim

Instructions:
- ○ Choose to use the wide or the narrow part of the tie.
- ○ Attach tie to necklace by tying it around the necklace as you would a regular tie.
- ○ Adjust it to desired length so the back excess can be cut off.
- ○ Cut the back piece shorter than the front for a finished look.
- ○ Secure tie by sewing or using fabric glue.
- ○ Wear tie or embellish further.

Refashioned T-shirt 101

About the program:

T-shirts can be refashioned in many ways. With a few snips here and there, that boring white T-shirt can be your next "go to" fashion piece. *Generation T* by Megan Nicolay (Workman Publishing, 2006) is a great book to have in your collection and will jump-start the teens to creating new looks. Or try the following no-sew projects to get things started.

Suggested number of participants: 10–25

Suggested program length: 1½ hours

Publicity: If you do not anticipate finding old T-shirts in a secondhand store, you should ask participants to bring an old T-shirt to the program.

Before the program date:

- • Gather and purchase supplies:
  - ○ Old T-shirt
  - ○ Fabric scissors

Day of the program:

- Instructions:
  - If the T-shirt has a collar, cut off the collar by simply cutting along the hem. You can choose to cut the neckline further if you want a different neckline or if your T-shirt has no collar.
  - Cut out the cuff in both sleeves by following the hemline. You will use these pieces for the bow ties on each sleeve.
  - Cut a slit in the top of the sleeve from the shoulder to the end of the sleeve. Pinch the shoulder sleeves together.
  - Using the sleeve off-cuts from the previous step, tie around the shoulder into a bow.
  - Website: http://www.generation-t.com/

Art at Your Heels: Shoes Fashion and Art

About this program:

Do you have an old pair of shoes that you are tired of but are still suitable to "recycle," meaning are still wearable? You can refashion this ugly pair of shoes and create a wearable work of art by adding paint, glitter, feathers, rhinestones, or gemstone to the shoes.

Suggested number of participants: 10–25

Suggested program length: 1–1½ hours

Publicity: On the publicity, ask teens to bring a pair of shoes that they don't like and that their parents don't mind them decorating. If you have already done (or plan to do) the Sneaky Sneakers program mentioned in Chapter 5, suggest they not bring sneakers but another type of shoe.

Supplies:

- Buttons, old jewelry, lace
- Glitter and gemstones
- Colored germinate Sharpies
- Heavy-duty glue
- Acrylic paint and acrylic sealer

Instructions:

- Glue on decorations.
- Decorate with paint or Sharpies.
- Get friends to sign them or make doodles.
- Write a favorite quote.

Websites for inspiration:

- Etsy, women's painted shoes (http://www.etsy.com/search?includes%5B0%5D=tags &q=handpainted+shoes&ref=related&page=1)
- http://www.funkytrend.com/tag/funky-shoes/

BIBLIOGRAPHY

Nonfiction

AlternaCrafts by Jessica Vitkus, Stewart, Tabori & Chang, 2005

Demin Decorating: Designer Gilitz for Denim, Includes 35 Step-by-Step Projects by Alison Spanyol, Cico, 2007

Eco-Chic Fashion Paradox by Sandy Black, St. Martin's Griffin, 2008

Fashion Geek: Clothes Accessories Tech by Diana Eng, North Light Books, 2009

Geek Chic by Margie Palatini, HarperCollins, 2009

Generation T: Beyond Fashion: 120 New Ways to Transform a T-shirt by Megan Nicolay, Workman Publishing Company, 2009

Girls Gone Green by Lynn Hirshfield, Penguin Group, 2010,

Jazzy Jeans by Michey Baskett, Sterling, 2007

Just for the Frill of It: 25 Flirty, Fabulous Styles to Make from Clothes you Already Own by Sonya Nimri, Watson-Guptill, 2007

Little Green Dresses: 50 Original Patterns to Repurpose Dresses, Tops, Skirts and More by Tinq Sparkles, Tauton Press, 2010

101 Tees: Restyle + Refashion + Revamp by Cathie Filian, Lark Crafts, 2011

Pulp Fiction: Perfect Paper Projects by Mark Montano, Design Originals, 2011

Refashion Bags by Faith Blakeney, Potter Craft, 2009

Rip It by Elissa Meyrich, Fireside, 2006

Rubbish!: Reuse Your Refuse by Kate Shoup, Wiley Publishing, 2008

Second-Time Cool: The Art of Chopping Up a Sweater by Anna-Stina, Annick Press Limited, 2005

Subversive Seamster: Transform Thrift Store Threads Into Street Couture by Mellissa Alvarado, Taunton Press, 2007

World of Geekcrafts: Step-by-Step Instructions for 25 Super-Cool Craft Projects by Susan Beal, Chronicle Books, 2011

Resources for Librarians

Born-Again Vintage: 25 Ways to Deconstruct, Reinvent, + Recycle Your Wardrobe by Bridgett Artise, Potter Craft, 2008

Style Naturally: The Savvy Shopping Guide to Sustainable Fashion and Beauty by Summer Rayne Oakes, Chronicle Books, 2008

    This is an adult book but is an excellent guide to Websites for sustainable fashion.

Several libraries have presented Alternative or Green Fashion Shows; check out their programs on the Internet:

In 2007, *Voya* chose Fayetteville, AK's, Alternative Fashion show, the 2007 most valuable teen program; check out http://www.jeninelillian.com/programs/teen-alternative-fashion-show-fayetteville-ar/

Check out the use of newspaper, plastic bags, and duct tape in Project Metamorphosis by the Yorba Linda Library teens at http://www.flickr.com/photos/yorbalindalibrary.

Lake County Library System just had their "Trash to Fashion Contest." Have a look at the creative outfits created by their teens at http://www.mylakelibrary.org/teens/photo_gallery .aspx?catid=137.

Lake County also has a very interesting Teen page with a whole section devoted to "Fashion is the New Me." Check out http://www.mylakelibrary.org/teens/default.aspx.

"Green Teen Fashion" by Jennifer Stickles, *Voya*, October 2011, p. 35c

8

Time Traveler

Recently, vintage or old-school clothing has become very popular. With many television programs based in past decades, teens are being exposed to the fashions from these periods. When celebrities began to search out the vintage and thrift shops for clothes that were well made and had flair and character, it became okay to shop in thrift stores and vintage shops. However, everything your teens wear should not be old-school or vintage clothing; if it is, it becomes a costume. Instead, help them combine vintage with modern. This makes the vintage stand out and be interesting.

PROGRAMS

Who Wore What When?

About the program:

Who Wore What When? is a program that will test teens' knowledge of which celebrity wore what through the twentieth and twenty-first centuries. While this is, as described, an active program, it could also be a passive program if you use the ideas but take out the things done during an in-the-library program.

Suggested number of participants: 10–25

Suggested program length: 1½–2 hours

Publicity: In the publicity for this program, you must suggest that teens come in one to two weeks before the actual program to complete their quiz. This will help you determine the number of participants you might have the day of the program.

Before the program date:

- Print Appendix W "Fashion Icons Numbered Chairs Pictures and Questions" to use for a beginning activity.
- Prepare questions from Appendix X for the "Fashion Designers Trivia Numbered Chairs" game for a quiz here.
- Collect books for display.
- Determine how many activities you will have and then purchase the materials below for Vintage Jewelry Remake, Bejeweled Picture Frames, or Beaded Bookmarks.

- Collect inexpensive vintage jewelry from thrift stores, or check online for jewelry by the bag for the Vintage Jewelry Remake.
- Purchase picture frames for the Bejeweled Picture Frames activity. If you do not have glue, purchase that also.
- Buy plastic wire for the Beaded Bookmarks activity.
- Decorate the program area with pictures of fashion icons and clothes or pictures of clothes from the different decades. Do not forget to include clothes for guys and male fashion icons.
- Purchase snacks that were from the different decades. Many of the popular snacks, cookies, and candies are still available in stores and online. The Web addresses for two companies are http://www.sweetservices.com/nostalgic-retro-candy/ and http://www.oldtimecandy.com/.
- Begin Famous Fashion Icon Contest in the library
  - Two to three weeks before the program, have a contest to see who can correctly identify the fashion icons from 1900–2010.
  - Enlarge photographs of famous fashion icons and decorate the Teen area. Give each photograph a number.
- Place answer sheets in the Teen Zone with instructions on the contest. Decorate the program area with pictures of fashion icons and clothes or pictures of clothes from the different decades. Do not forget to include clothes for guys and male fashion icons.
  - When a teen has filled in all the spaces, the answer sheet is turned in to the designated area. Each answer sheet will have the teen's name, date and time, and initials of the staff person accepting the answer sheet.
  - Winner will be announced at the program.

<u>Day of the program</u>

- Choose either "Fashion Icons Numbered Chairs Pictures and Questions" (Appendix W) or "Fashion Designers Trivia Numbered Chairs" (Appendix X): (30 minutes to 45 minutes depending on attendance)
  - After the game, talk about words, styles, and people that may become the icons for the 2010s.
- Vintage Jewelry Remake:
  <u>Instructions</u>:
  - Take charms and pendants from old jewelry and make a new charm bracelet.
- Bejeweled Picture Frames
  <u>Instructions</u>:
  - Take a plain picture frame and glue the fronts of old earrings, removing the back first, and old pins to make a glitz frame.
- Beaded Bookmarks
  <u>Instructions</u>:
  - Take an 18" piece of wire and make a flat spiral at the top of the wire like a lollipop.
  - Begin stringing beads randomly from the bottom.
  - Continue with twists and spirals, adding more beads as desired.

- ○ End with another spiral at the bottom of the bookmark.
- ○ Use the spiral at the top of the bookmark as a paper clip marker while positioning the rest of the bookmark on the outside cover.

Vintage Fashion Film Festival

About the program:

Many movie stars reflect the fashions of the era of either their movies or the year that the movie was made. The film festival will show clips from movies and then discuss clothes that were worn and what they had to say about the culture of that time.

Suggested number of participants: 10–50 for a good discussion. The audience should be small enough for everyone to have an opportunity to speak but not so small that the discussion isn't lively.

Suggested program length: 1½– 2 hours

Before the program date:

- Select films from the 1920s to the 1980s that have stars that were considered the best dressed from that era. Allow enough time to get permission to screen these clips.
- After watching the films, select a couple of scenes that highlight the fashions and that highlight both women's and men's styles.
- Find books in the collection with pictures of the stars and the fashions to use as a reference and for teens to look at.
- For discussion, become familiar with some of the events that were happening during those periods that affected style and fashion.

Day of the program:

- Before showing each clip, set the stage by explaining when the movie was made, who the stars were in the film, and a little about what else was going on in the world at that time so the teens are prepared for the discussion below.
- Ask the teens to pay attention to the costumes in the clip and to think about how those clothes might be used with the current fashions.
- After seeing the clip, stop and have a discussion on the style of the clothing. Look not only at the dresses or suits but at the accessories, shoes, hairstyles, colors, and fabrics.
- Talk about what was going on in the world that might have affected the styles.
- Ask the teens if there were items that they might wear today. How could they mix an article of clothing, shoes, or accessories with something they already have in their closets?

"Clothes from Yesterday" Fashion Show

About the program:

Treasures are often hidden in people's closets just waiting to be seen again. A vintage fashion show is a great multigenerational program. Teens will have an opportunity to talk to grandparents about the clothes they wore. And don't forget the parents—they may have clothes with stories to tell.

<u>Suggested number of participants</u>: Unlimited

<u>Suggested program length</u>: 1½–2 hours

<u>Publicity</u>: This program involves many in the community and should have the potential for seniors and other adult patrons who come to the library. For this reason, it has excellent possibilities for a great deal of positive coverage in the media and the newspaper; radio station and television station staff should be involved early in the planning stages and during the program, too.

<u>Before the program date</u>:

- Connect with senior organizations in the community and explain the ideas you have for a "Clothes from Yesterday" program. Ask about visiting their locations at a time when you might have a crowd, perhaps at the beginning of another activity, to explain the project. Some of the seniors might still be able to get into their fashions and would make great models. Others might be willing to loan clothes that the teens could model. If clothes are too fragile to be worn, ask if they could be displayed at the fashion show.
- For the clothes that are being displayed, ask the seniors to be on hand to talk to the teens. They can talk about where they wore the outfits and what made it so special that they kept them.
- Men may have military uniforms that the teen guys would enjoy talking about.
- It's not just about clothes but also the accessories: jewelry, purses, and shoes.
- Other sources for seniors would be library customers, churches, and the families of teens council members.
- Purchase food for refreshments. Remember that the audience will be multigenerational, so have food that appeals to a wide audience. Some ideas for refreshments would include food that was popular in different decades. Ask your seniors for some examples. One is the molded Jell-O salad, which was popular in the 1950s. Jell-O can still be found in most grocery stores. Three historical cakes are Pineapple Upside Down Cake, Carrot Cake, and Angel Food Cake. The last two cakes remain very popular today. Print out the history of the dessert that you choose and place it near the dessert so everyone can see the history of the dessert.

<u>Day of the program</u>:

See "Introduction" about Fashion Shows for additional help.

- When teens and guests arrive, have trivia games available to get them in the mood. For some suggestions, see the Appendix L "Shoes thoughout History Trivia Quiz"; Appendix N "Famous Hats"; and Appendix R "Hair through History Trivia" for beginning suggestions.
- Arrange the clothes for display and have plenty of signs that say "Fragile, please do not touch."
- After the fashion show have a discussion about how clothes have changed over the years and the ways that they may change in the future.

<u>Resources</u>:

- http://www.texasmonthly.com/forum/main/article/4485 is not a library program but a good example of how to do a vintage fashion show.
- Bloomfield-Eastern Greene Public Library had a 1940s fashion show and has a very good pictorial at http://www.bloomfield.lib.in.us/2009/03/24/vintage-1940s-fashion-show-42608.

Mad about Vintage

<u>About the program</u>:

Many teens might be interested in vintage clothes but have no idea what is vintage and what is just old. Teens are probably not very good at choosing clothes to add to their closets. Many may never have thought about wearing something "old." Mad about Vintage will give teens information about what vintage is and which accessories to choose to incorporate vintage items into their wardrobe.

<u>Suggested number of participants</u>: 10–50

<u>Suggested program length</u>: 1–1½ hours

<u>Before the program date</u>:

- See "Introduction" for Finding Guest Speakers instructions.
- Arrange with the owner of a local vintage clothing store to be a guest speaker at the program. Another source for a speaker would be a local museum that has exhibits of vintage fashion.
- Ask both the vintage store owner and the museum staff member if they will bring examples of vintage fashion so that the teens can see what they are talking about.
- Ask them to explain how the vintage clothes can work with today's fashion.

<u>Day of the program</u>:

- A guest speaker
- Discussion of ways to wear vintage clothing

BIBLIOGRAPHY

Fiction

Cast Off Coven by Juliet Blackwell, Signet, 2010
Larceny and Lace by Annette Blair, Vintage Magic Mystery series, Berkley, 2009
Secret Lives of Dress by Erin McKean, 5 Spot, 2011
The Time-Traveling Fashionista by Bianca Turetsky, Poppy, 2011
Vintage Veronica by Erica Perl, Knopf Books for Young Readers, 2010.

(Most of these titles are adult books; however, they are appropriate for teens but maybe not for 'tweens.)

Nonfiction

Born Again Vintage: 25 Ways to Deconstruct, Reinvent, and Recycle Your Wardrobe by Bridgett Artise, Potter Craft, 2008

DIY Fashion by Selena Francis-Bryden, Laurence King Publishing, London, England, 2010

The Fashion File: Advice, Tips and Inspiration from the Costume Designer of Mad Men by Monica Corcoran Harel, Grand Central Life Style, 2010

Fashion 101: A Crash Course in Clothing by Erika Stalder, Zest Books, 2008

Little Green Dresses: 50 Original Patterns for Repurposed Dresses, Tops, Skirts, and More by by Tina Sparkles, Taunton Press, 2010

Making Vintage Bags: 20 Original Sewing Patterns for Vintage Bags and Purses by Emma Brennan, Guild of Master Craftsmen, 2006

Making Vintage Jewellery by Emma Brennan, Guild of Master Craftsmen, 2006

Retro Knits: Cool Vintage Patterns for Men, Women, and Children from the 1900s Through the 1970s by Kari Cornell, Voyageur Press, 2008

Shopping for Vintage: The Definitive Guide to Vintage Fashion by Funmi Odulate, St. Martin's, 2008

60s Fashion: Vintage Fashion and Beauty Aids by Laura Schooling, Heimann, 2007

Vintage Craft Workshop by Cathi Callahan, Chronicle Book, 2011

Vintage Fashion Accessories by Stacy Lo Albo, Krause Publications, 2009

Vintage Hairstyling: Retro Styles with Step-by-Step Techniques by Lauren Rennells, HRST Books, 2009

9

Manga Fashionistas

Anime and Manga are very popular among teens. A perfect way to highlight your library's collection is by offering related programming. Cosplay (short for costume play) is the art of dressing as a character from a Manga series. Cosplay is not just the fashions but also hair and makeup. The hairstyles are often cut in many layers, choppy, and very straight. Although the styles are very distinctive, there are ways to personalize the look for individual tastes. Cosplay can also include characters from comic superheroes and fiction book characters, such as *Batman* and *Hunger Games*. In this chapter the focus is on Anime and Manga characters. Anime 101 is a glossary of popular Anime and Manga words and their definitions. It is also a list of some of the most popular series.

Anime 101

Anime—Japanese animation. The term can also include styles of animation that are similar to Japanese animation.

Manga—Japanese comics. This is a broad term that may be used to describe a particular style of graphic novels that are similar to Japanese comics.

Otaku—Means "fan" in Japanese. This term is proudly used by many Anime and Manga fans. Use this term with caution because in Japan it has a more negative connotation.

Shojo—The story lines are often directed to a female demographic although many of these titles also have a large male following.

Shonen—The story lines are often directed to a male demographic.

Popular Series

Naruto
Fruits Basket
Inuyasha
Deathnote
Bleach
Pokemon
Ouran High School Host Club
One Piece
Full Metal Alchemist
Dragon Ball Z

PROGRAMS

AnimeCon (Anime Convention)

<u>About the program</u>:

An Anime convention is a gathering place that focuses on Anime, Manga, and the Japanese culture. Conventions across the United States can be attended to provide ideas for activities at your AnimeCon. These conventions usually have speakers, activities, and industry retailers who exhibit their products. Combine several of the following programs to create your own library AnimeCon for your teens. If an AnimeCon is not feasible, any of the activities can be used for individual programs.

<u>Suggested number of participants</u>: This number will be determined by the amount of space available in your library. To create a real convention atmosphere, prepare to have a large gathering.

<u>Suggested program length</u>: ½ day–full day.

<u>Before the program date</u>:

- Put together swag bags (free stuff) for the teens to take with them. Write to Anime publishers asking if they have any free items that you can have to promote their titles that they are willing to donate to the AnimeCon.
- Contact any local gaming businesses or media stores that sell Anime and ask them for donations.
- Determine how many activities you wish to have and purchase supplies for each.
- Buy popcorn and decide how to pop it.
- Purchase Japanese food to serve for refreshments: sushi, pot stickers, ramen noodles, sobe noodles, or anything else Japanese that the teens might like to try.

<u>Day of the program</u>:

- Anime viewing, showing half-hour segments of Anime programs, with popcorn.
- Drawing contest—teens can create a costume for a favorite Anime character. These will be judged, and the winner announced at the end of the program.
- The art area can also include origami, coloring sheets, and Shrinky Dinks for key chains or earrings.
- If the library has a button machine, or access to one, create buttons of favorite Anime characters. Save discarded graphic novels or magazines to use for graphics.
- Provide an area for role-playing games.
- Every half hour play a numbered chairs trivia game.
- A costume fashion show, in which everyone who arrives in costume has a chance to model their costumes. The audience can vote for their favorite costumes. Have different categories: 1) best hairdo, 2) best in keeping with the character, 3) best original costume, and 4) best overall costume.
- If there is someone in the community who speaks Japanese, invite him or her to teach the teens some basic Japanese words and demonstrate Japanese writing. Give the teens an opportunity to create a greeting card written in Japanese.
- Candy Sushi (see program below for instructions).

- Photo area where teens can have their picture taken with teens in costumes.
- Anime book or comic swap.

<u>Refreshments</u>:

- Have a variety of Japanese food.

<u>Resources</u>:

"Host Your Own Anime Convention" by Maureen DeLaughter, *Voya*, October 21, 238–239.

Candy Sushi

<u>About the program</u>:

This program will become a favorite for your teens because it enables them to be creative and enjoy the fruits of their labor. While Candy Sushi is a great program to offer alone, it would tie-in great with any of your Anime programming. Think about offering this one at your AnimeCon. Many "how-to" online food programs show how to make candy sushi using a thin sheet of rice crispy treats that can be filled with fruit strip and other candies, then rolled up like sushi. We found that using Twinkies works better in a library setting, especially if you have limited kitchen access or other restrictions. Mini powdered donuts and pound cake also work well as "rice" to make a variety of sushi-inspired candy.

<u>Before the program date</u>:

<u>Supplies</u>:

- Twinkies
- Mini powdered donuts and pound cake (optional)
- Assorted fruity decorative candies
- Green fruit leather (fruit roll-ups work great)
- Sweet shredded coconut
- Swedish fish
- Plastic knives
- Paper plates or small take-out boxes
- Chop sticks

<u>Day of the program</u>:

<u>Directions</u>:

- Cut Twinkies into round slices about an inch tall.
- Cut fruit rollups in strips to be long enough and wide enough to wrap around the Twinkie pieces.
- Place candies into the cream filling to represent the sushi filling.
- Place Twinkie rolls on a plate or in a take-out box.
- Garnish with strips of dried mango to resemble pickled ginger, if you wish.
- Serve with chopsticks.

Sushi using mini powdered donuts:

- Cut the powdered donuts in half and place cut side down.
- Lay one Swedish fish on top and wrap a strip of green fruit leather around it.
- To make sushi using pound cake, cut pound cake into small rectangles. Layer Swedish fish or other candies on top, then wrap a strip of green fruit leather around it.

Also see *The Secret Life of Food*, by Clare Crespo, Hyperion, 2005

Anime/Manga Book Swap

About the program:

Invite teens to bring their Manga comic books or Anime movies and swap them for "new" titles. You may want to start gathering books in advance and decide the rules for swap. It could be an even trade or a swap in exchange for a book review, or you could just allow teens to pick out whatever they would like to read next even if they didn't bring a book for the swap. Try to add some additional titles from your donations, advanced readers, or discards because the demand will always be greater than the supply.

A book swap can be a passive program. Have a small space near the teen desk where teens can bring in graphic novels and swap for another (new) book. This can be an ongoing passive program or can be advertised for a month leading up to another Anime program.

Suggested number of participants: Up to 30

Suggested program length: 45 minutes–1½ hours

Before the program date:

- See "Introduction" for information about Swaps.
- When discarding the well-used copies in your collection, keep them for the swap. Write to publishers, asking for preview copies and/or a donation of titles.
- Decide on rules for swapping to include in the publicity.
- Decide how the books and DVDs will be organized.
- Count the number of books and DVDs that you will have at the beginning.
- See AnimeCon above for food suggestions for refreshments and purchase.
- Create an opening activity: see Appendix Y "Anime Guys with Black Hair"; or Appendix Z "Anime Trivia."

Day of the program:

- For statistical purposes have a volunteer at the door to tally the number of books that are brought in. When teens leave, the volunteer will tally how many books each teen takes out. This will be necessary if there is a limit on how many books each teen can take.
- Ask the teens to bring their books and DVDs a couple of weeks prior to the program so there will be books for those who arrive first. Keep some of the books in the back to replenish the selection throughout the program.

- Have Japanese snacks for refreshments.

What's New in Manga

About the program:

Invite your book supplier or a marketing representative to make a presentation about What's New and Coming Soon in the world of Manga. Many publishers have PowerPoint presentations that they are willing to share with librarians. As you run through the new titles, this would be an excellent time to ask your teens what titles they would like to see in the collection. Ask the marketing representative if they have any bookmarks or related materials that they can provide for the teens. You should invite your school librarians to attend this session also.

Suggested number of participants: 20–50

Suggested program length: 45 minutes–1½ hours

Day of the program:

- Speaker
- In addition to the presentation, preview a new Anime DVD.

Manga Book Speed Discussing

About the program:

The Wichita Public Library had a great idea for a book-sharing program based on the format used in a Speed Dating evening. A spin on this program would be to limit the books discussed to Manga titles, either sharing a favorite series or one special book from a series.

Suggested number of participants: 10–50

Suggested program length: 1½–2 hours

Publicity: Include in the publicity for each teen to bring a favorite Manga "book talk" for other teens.

Before the program date:

- Prepare a bookmark. On one side have a list of the newest graphic novels in the library, and on the other side have a place for teens to make notes about good titles they want to remember to read.
- Sharpen pencils for teens to use to write the titles they want to read.
- Plan the program well in advance, so the newest Manga titles or volumes of popular titles can be ordered and available for teens to check out the day of the program.

Day of the program:

- Set up room with tables, four chairs per table, two at each end. If teens prefer, they could sit on the floor facing each other.
- Set up a display of the newest Manga titles available.

- Welcome the teens to Speed Discussing for Manga Books. Announce upcoming events.
- Give teens a demonstration on how to do a book talk.
- Teens then pair up and find a comfortable place to sit. If the teens don't know each other, have them introduce themselves. Give them about two minutes to get to know their partners. Ring the bell.
- When the bell is rung, there are three minutes to tell your partner about the book that was brought to share. At the end of three minutes, the bell will ring again, and the other person will have three minutes to share their book. If there is time, the two people can ask each other question or make comments.
- If they are interested in reading the book shared, have them write it on their Books to Read Next bookmark.
- At the end of the second three minutes, the bell will ring, and both teens will have one minute to find a new partner. The process will continue for three three-minute sessions, or approximately 30 minutes. At the end of three sessions, call for a break.
- Have a 20-minute break for refreshments.
- Return for three more sessions. If the teens are having a good time, extend for an additional 30 minutes.

Anime Screening

About the program:

This is a screen showing of the latest Anime title with popcorn and other goodies.

Suggested number of participants: 10–50

Suggested program length: 1–2 hours

Before the program date:

- Ask one of your more knowledgeable teens to host the screening and be prepared to provide interesting tidbits and background about the Anime.
- You should also be prepared to discuss the similarities and differences between the same title in Anime (DVD) and Manga. Check out Operation Anime (http://www.operationanime.com), which will provide you with Anime DVDs for your Anime screening in exchange for completed feedback surveys.
- Make sure you request performance rights for any DVD you decide to show.
- Purchase popcorn and make sure you have an easy way to pop it.
- Paper bowls for popcorn.

Day of the program:

- Show DVD.
- Distribute and collect feedback surveys.

Sewing 101—Cosplay Style

About this program:

Learn how you can take ordinary clothes and turn them into cosplay masterpieces. Invite teens to bring clothing or costumes from past Halloweens to make new cosplay costumes. This could be a two-part program in which the teens will make their costumes beforehand, then wear them for the convention and/or Cosplay runway.

Suggested number of participants: 10–20

Suggested program length: 2 hours

Before the program date:

- Make sure you have the supplies needed.

Supplies:
- Sewing machine
- Fabrics, fabric trim, and other sewing embellishments
- Glue guns and fabric glue sticks
- Pictures of various Anime characters
- Iron-on patches
- Scissors
- Iron
- Fusible webbing

Cosplay Runway

About the program:

Suggested number of participants: About 10–15 for runway participants

Suggested program length: 1–1½ hours

Before the program date:

- See "Introduction" for more information on Fashions Shows.
- Checkout Cumberland County Public Library & Information Center at http://www.youtube.com/watch?v=8AX8s2frmgQ on Cosplay Runway.

Cosplay Fleece Hat

About the program:

Keep warm all winter with these easy-to-make fleece hats. Fleece is both a stretchable and a forgiving fabric, thus making for an easy no-sew project. Offer patterns that feature animals and floppy ears to appeal to your Manga fans. These hats can be used to create a fun-filled cosplay teen program.

<u>Suggested number of participants</u>: 10–25 (teens will need lots of direction with using patterns)

<u>Suggested program length</u>: 2 hours

<u>Before the program date</u>:

- Purchase supplies.

    <u>Supplies</u>:

    - Soft tape measure
    - Fleece fabric
    - Felt in various colors
    - Pins
    - Fabric glue
    - Scissors
    - Hat templates
    - Fabric paint or markers
    - Tracing paper

<u>Instructions</u>:

- Have teens measure the circumference of their heads (around their ears) to determine the width of the hat.
- Cut out fabric from a basic template and invite teens to customize the pattern.
- Glue pattern right sides together along the inside of these edges.
- Turn the hat right side out.
- Cut out designs from felt.
- Affix shapes using more fabric glue. For tiny shapes, if it's easier for you, draw them onto the hat later with the fine-tip markers or fabric paints.

Pikachu Hat Tutorial

http://browse.deviantart.com/?qh=&section=&q=fleece+hat+tutorial#/d1iwjy4

Anime-Inspired Buttons

<u>About this program</u>:

Buttons, pins, and badges are always popular with teens. These are versatile accessories that can be worn on a shirt, a backpack, a hat, on shoes, or even on a headband. Buttons come in various shapes and sizes although the round 1 to 1½ inch is the most popular with teens. If you are fortunate enough to own a badge maker, then check with the manufacturer for needed badge-making supplies; otherwise, use existing badges to customize or update them. Inspired buttons can be used as an activity in a number of programs.

<u>Suggested number of participants</u>: 10–25

<u>Suggested program length</u>: 45 minutes–1 hour

<u>Before the program date</u>:

- Purchase or gather supplies needed.

<u>Supplies</u>:

- Badge maker
- Corresponding supplies/old buttons (check secondhand stores or discount stores; you may find a surplus of Christmas-themed buttons on sale after the holidays for a great price).
- Decoupage medium (only if you do not have a badge machine). Note: there are different types of finishes. Glossy works well for this project.
- Small artwork: Advise teens about the size of button and how the artwork will wrap a little around the sides.
  - Sometimes the badge-making company will include blanks that can be used or software to make custom badges.
  - Discarded magazines or Manga would work well with this project.
  - Various colors of ink pens and precut paper circles. Teens can choose to create their own fan art.

<u>Instructions</u>:

Since the pallet is small, this project should take only about 15–30 minutes. Teens can have an opportunity to make multiple buttons and they will ask to.
  - Use decoupage to adhere artwork to existing badge.
  - Saturate artwork so that it will be smooth around the back side.
  - Cover entire surface with decoupage. The more coats you use, the glossier it will be.
  - Insert artwork into badge machine and follow machine instructions.

Earrings/Zipper Pull

<u>About the program</u>:

Fans love to show their love of Manga. Have them create accessories based on their favorite series or characters. Discarded Manga titles and magazines will give this project a professional finish.

<u>Suggestion number of participants</u>: 15–30

<u>Suggested program length</u>: 1–2 hours

<u>Before the program date</u>:

- Purchase the needed supplies for earrings.
- Supplies for earrings
  - Jump rings in various sizes (larger ones work best for this)
  - Lobster closures
  - Chipboard (precut in various small shapes, about 1 inch sized) for jewelry
  - Discarded Manga books and magazines

- ○ Scissors
- ○ Decoupage glue
- ○ Foam brushes
- ○ Jewelry awl or dremel to make holes for jump rings

<u>Instructions</u>:

- ○ Select and cut out artwork from books. Try to choose artwork that will fit chipboard shapes.
- ○ Glue to chipboard and seal by adding more glue to the surface of picture.
- ○ Drill a hole near edge to accommodate a jump ring.
- ○ Add earring findings to create earrings or lobster closure to create zipper pull.

Amigurumi—Cute Stuffed Toys

<u>About this program</u>:

Introduce the industry of textiles through knitting or crocheting. Amigurumi is the Japanese art of combining knitting (or crocheting) with doll making. Many amigurumi patterns are of animals and other characters with no other function than to be "cute." This is a great way to get your teens to pick up knitting because the projects are fun and easy to create. You have many resources to choose from to find great patterns. Try this program if you are comfortable with knitting or see a large interest in it in your community. This program can lead to other knitting programs in which you can create great accessories, such as hats or scarves.

<u>Suggested number of participants</u>: 10–15 (keep it small if everyone is a novice at crocheting or knitting)

<u>Suggested program length</u>: 2 hours

<u>Before the program date</u>:

- • Collect or buy supplies.

Supplies:

- ○ Knitting Needles or Crochet Hooks
- ○ Yarn
- ○ Patterns

See bibliography below for patterns and instructions.

Amigurumi by Lan-Anh Bui, 2010

Amigurumi Toy Box: Cute Crocheted Friends by Ana Paula Rimoli, 2011

The Complete Idiot's Guide to Amigurumi by June Gilbank, 2010

Super Cute: 25 Amigurumi Animals by Annie Obaachan, 2009 (This author has many other great titles.)

Cosplay Information, Pictures and Resources

Cosplay.com—http://www.cosplay.com— Vast forums and lots of users to help with questions. Also has a store and picture galleries.

Cosplay Lab—http://www.cosplaylab.com—A great number of resources and galleries, and a costume commission directory.

The Costumer's Manifesto—http://www.costumes.org—Directory of all sorts of different costume styles.

Cosplay Closet Tips—http://www.cosplaycloset.com—Lots of good tips from a professional costumer.

American Cosplay Paradise—http://www.acparadise.com—Large directory of female costumers nationwide.

BIBLIOGRAPHY

Girl to Grrrl Manga: How to Draw the Hottest Shojo Manga by Colleen Doran, Impact, 2006
How to Cosplay Graphic Volume 1: Transformation and Special-effects Make-up by Graphic-Sha, Graphic-Sha Publishing Company, 2009
Shojo Fashion Manga Art School: How to Draw Cool Looks and Characters by Irene Flores, Impact, 2009
Survival of the Fiercest by Anne Carey, *HarperTeen,* 2009
Tokyo Look Book: Stylish To Spectacular, Goth to Gyaru, Sidewalk To Catwalk by Philomena, Keet Kodansha, USA, 2007
Wagashi Sudo by Kumiko Sudo, Reckling Press, 2007

Other Resources

Cosp Mailing List—largest Yahoo! group for cosplay
Cosplay ML—another Yahoo! group for cosplay
http://www.Cosplaysupplies.com—store for ordering costume supplies (Canadian)
Costumer's Manifesto—site with a lot of resource links
Faerie Fingers—http://faerie-fingers.com/—sells cosplay patterns
Katie Bair's—http://www.katiebair.com/wigs.html—custom wig designs for cosplayers
Lunar Dragon—http://www.anichive.com/lunardragon/—costume commission site
Patterns of Time—period renaissance and traditional Asian-style patterns
Samurai Game—traditional Japanese armor and clothing resource
The Other Me—make a duct tape model of yourself!

APPENDIX A

Fashion Terms

A-line—dress/skirt shape that is narrower at the top and gently flaring out to the bottom, following the shape of the letter A. Flattering for bottom-heavy figures.

Accent—is a distinctive feature that accentuates the look and style of a garment. Can be a touch of color, embroidery, etc., that makes a designer's work look unique.

Appliqué—refers to stitching in which a design is created by sewing pieces of fabric (or other materials) together onto a fabric background.

Baby Doll—is a short nightgown with hem that terminates just below the hip. A baby doll is longer than a cropped top but shorter than a chemise.

Baby Doll Dress—above the knee empire-waist dress, modeled according to the baby doll, often gathered at the top and adorned with lace, appliqué, ruffles, bows, etc.

Back Drape—a length of material, attached either at the shoulder or the waist that flows over the back to floor length. In some cases, it's removable.

Ballerina Flat or Ballet Flat—is a flat shoe with a thin, skid-proof sole, often with a drawstring, an elastic top line, or a modern design. This is a staple for the city girl.

Bandeau/Tube Top—is a strapless, band-shaped bodice.

Basque Waist/V-Waist—is a dropped waist that starts at, or just below, the natural waistline and dips in the center, creating a V shape.

Bateau Neck/Boat Neck—a high, wide, neckline that runs straight across the front and back, meeting at the shoulders; it has the same depth in the front and back.

Bell Sleeve—is a long sleeve that flares at the bottom like a bell.

Bias—is a textile term used when a garment is cut at an angle to the warp (horizontal yarns) and weft (vertical yarns) of a fabric. This is used to create garments that closely follow the curves of the body.

Bohemian—a trend that describes a free-spirited attitude towards fashion with a lot of feminine details including flounces, ties, ribbons, ruffles, and embroidery. It can also be called poetic, romantic, and folkloric in style. Originally comes from the Eastern European culture.

Boot-Cut—refers to trousers or jeans that are cut below the belly button and flare slightly from the knees to the ankles to accommodate any type of footwear.

Broomstick Dress—a dress (or skirt) characterized by its numerous pleats and crinkled material.

Bubble Skirt—a voluminous skirt, somewhat resembling a balloon.

Bustier—a sleeveless, strapless top or dress held in place by boning, elastic, or stretch fabrics. It is designed to help shape and enhance the bustline.

Buti—a small embroidery motif, usually floral, but can be paisley/mango shaped or of other shapes as well.

Camisole—is a short, sleeveless garment for a woman, which often feels like lingerie.

Cap Sleeves—a small, short sleeve that sits exactly on the shoulder or falling just onto the arm.

Capri Pants—three-quarter-length pants designed to hit mid-calf, first popularized on the Isle of Capri.

Cardigan Jacket—is usually a collarless sweater or jacket that opens the full length of the center front.

Cargo Style—pants or shorts with patch pocket or bellows pocket with a flap (usually a button flap) and made of cargo material; the classics are in green or beige colors.

Chanel Style—anything that is elegant, simple, and easy to wear. The classics are little black dresses and suits with multi-chain jewelry. The style is named after Coco Chanel, the French couturier.

Charmeuse—is a man-made, shiny, silk-like fabric.

Chemise—usually a short nightgown hemmed below the hip and above the knee. Held up by thin spaghetti straps, the gown should fit snugly at the bust and upper torso and fall loosely and flow past the hips.

Chiffon—a lightweight, plain-weave, sheer fabric made with very fine, tightly twisted yarns. It is very strong, despite its filmy look.

Clog—is a casual shoe on a wooden base, usually with a closed toe and an open back.

Cotton Poplin—medium weight, durable, textured fabric made with cotton or cotton blends.

Cotton/Spandex—a blend of lightweight, breathable fabric made with durable, stretchable, manmade fibers of polyurethane and natural cottons.

Cowl Neck—a neckline featuring a piece of material attached to a garment at the neck which is draped loosely and hangs from shoulder to shoulder at the front neckline or back.

Crepe—is fabric which is characterized by a crinkled and puckered surface or soft, mossy finish. It comes in different weights and degrees of sheerness.

Crew Neck—a round neck with ribbed banding that fits close to the base of the neck.

Crochet—is a technique for making a garment or shoe with a lacelike effect, involving a hook and a yarn.

Cropped Top/Jacket—an article of clothing where the hem is cut just above the waist.

Day to Evening—is a look that can take you from a day in the office straight to a night on the town with just minor changes, such as adding or changing accessories.

Décolleté—is a very low-cut neckline, falling in a V-shape to below the bust, giving you a plunging neckline; this look often reveals the shoulders and back as well. This is also a name for a woman's neck and cleavage area.

Deconstruction—is a term used to describe clothing that has been taken apart and put back together in a new, unexpected way, or looks unfinished and raw, as though it may be deteriorating.

Dolman Sleeve—cut as an extension of the bodice, the dolman sleeve is designed without a socket for the shoulder, creating a deep, wide armhole that reaches from the waist to a narrowed wrist.

Double-Breasted—a style of closure in a jacket that has one edge of a garment overlapping another with a double row of buttons or other fasteners.

Drape—describes the hang or fall of fabric when made into a garment.

Duster—a long, open, lightweight coat, with or without a button closure.

Empire Waist—is a waistline that begins just below the bust, designed with a high waist to create a flattering sweep.

Eyelet—is a type of fabric punched with decorative holes and embroidered with purl stitching.

Fabric Lining—the inner layer of fabric used to cover the inside of a garment. It is usually made of soft, smooth fabric, which adds to the outfit by making it more flattering and gives it extra protection.

Faux—is originally a French word meaning imitation or fake. It is most often used in connection with gems, pearls, leathers, and furs.

Finish—is the level of perfection with which a garment is completed. In the best garments, the inside will look as complete as the outside.

Flare Pants—pants that flare at the hem, also called bell-bottoms.

Formfitting—this is a style that closely skims the body and emphasizes the natural curves without being tight.

Gaucho—wide-legged pants or divided skirt reaching mid-calf.

Grain—a term used to describe the direction of the weft (vertical yarns). Clothes are traditionally cut on the grain, i.e., along the length of a fabric. "On the cross grain" refers to cutting fabric in the direction of the warp (horizontal yarns).

Halter—is a sleeveless top with a plunging neckline; the cut leaves the shoulders bare and is quite often backless.

Handkerchief Hem—a handkerchief hem falls in several graceful points to flatter all figures.

Haute Couture—french word for high fashion, which is handmade. Couture itself relates to dressmaking, sewing, or needlework while haute means elegant or high. The pieces require several fittings and are staggeringly expensive because they are one of a kind. To qualify as haute couture piece, a garment must follow several strict guidelines. For a label or business to qualify as a couture house, it must belong to Syndical Chamber for Haute Couture in France.

Hip-Huggers—are low-slung pants, skirt, or belt worn below the natural waist, creating the impression of a longer, leaner torso.

Ikat—is a handcraft in which the yarns are carefully tie-dyed in a particular design before they are woven together.

Inseam—the inside seam of a pant leg, dress, or skirt.

Jacquard—a raised design or pattern woven into a fabric, as opposed to being printed on the fabric.

Kaftan—is a full-length garment with elbow or full-length sleeves; now kaftans come in all lengths. Often highly embellished with embroidery and originated in the Middle East

Kimono—is a Japanese garment. The kimono sleeve is a wide sleeve cut in one piece with the main body of the garment and traditionally worn with a broad sash.

Kitten Heel—first popularized by actress Audrey Hepburn, this chic little heel is about one to two inches high with a feminine curve to it.

LBD or the Little Black Dress—is a classic, black cocktail dress that has become a fashion staple after being first introduced by Coco Chanel. It is reinvented every season but never goes out of style.

Linen—is a type of fabric that is cooler, stronger, and more absorbent than cotton. It is woven from threads made from the flax plant.

Lycra Spandex—is a trademark brand made by the Du Pont Corporation; it is a type of fabric known for its spandex, stretchy material.

Matte Jersey—is a fine-knitted fabric with a flat finish.

Mary Janes—traditionally styled after school children's shoes with a rounded toe and a flat heel, the chief characteristic of a Mary Jane is the strap over the top of the foot. Today Mary Janes can be of any heel height and are a staple for shoes designers.

Microfiber—is a fabric made of silky synthetic material, usually woven polyester.

Minimalism—is a look and a trend in design in which clothes are stripped down to their most basic elements. It is characterized by simple forms and basic color schemes.

Minis/Maxis—a mini is a very short skirt or dress falling mid-thigh or higher. It was invented by Mary Quant in the 1960s. The maxi refers to a full length skirt/dress, usually ankle length or longer.

Moccasin—soft, loafer-like leather shoe constructed with lacing to attach the sole portion to a U-shaped upper. It is often elaborately beaded and copied from designs of the Native Americans.

Mules—type of a shoe without any back strap.

Natural Waist—describes the natural curve of the body, which is the indentation between the hips and the rib-cage.

No-Waistline—leaving the waistband out of pants or a dress to achieve an elegant simplicity and a smoother silhouette.

Open Stitch—shown in woven or knitted fabrics that are loosely-stitched, achieving a semitransparency.

Organza—fine, sheer, lightweight, crisp fabric with a stiff feel. It crushes or musses fairly easily, but it is easily pressed. It is a dressy fabric and sometimes has a silvery sheen.

Paisley—is a fabric print rich in swirling designs, which can be either woven in or screened, and is based on fine Scottish wool fabrics designed in yarn-dyed colors.

Pea Coat—traditionally a heavy, warm, hip-length woolen jacket with a double-breasted front and a wide notched collar. It was originally worn by sailors in a navy blue color.

Peasant Top—romantic-style top, often characterized with a low neckline, ruffles, or free-flowing material.

Pencil Skirt—skirt with a straight line that falls at or below the knee with no flare or fullness at the hem or waistline.

Platform Heels—type of shoes with thick soles made of wood, cork, or plastic. They create the illusion of height without the discomfort of a regular arched heel.

Pleats—a technique used to create volume in a garment by folding fabric and stitching it down at the top of the fold. Types of pleats include knife pleats (all folds facing one direction), box pleats (two flat folds in opposite directions with edges of the fabric meeting underneath), and inverted pleats (similar to a box pleat but with the fullness on the outer side).

Picot—is a row of small loops woven along the edge of a fabric in ribbon or lace for a decorative effect.

Pieced—a look created by sewing several pieces of material together to form a garment, much like a quilt.

Pigment-Dyed—yarns colored with material of animal, vegetable, or mineral origin before they are spun into fabric.

Pin-tuck—narrow, sewn-down pleats, usually on the front of a garment.

Piqué—(pronounced "pee-kay") is a durable, knit, or woven fabric with raised lengthwise cords or squares which are part of the weave.

Plissé—a French word meaning gathering, folding, or pleating, it describes a fabric with a puckered surface.

Pointelle—is an open-holed stitch, usually in the shape of a V, flower, or a diamond.

Polo Dress—a long or knee-length dress designed as an extension of the classic cotton knit polo shirt.

Polyester—a wrinkle-resistant fabric made from synthetic materials.

Poncho—is a square and straight piece of fabric, usually waterproof, with an opening in the center for the head. Originally a Latin American garment in colorful woven fabrics that was used as outerwear.

Poplin—a finely ribbed fabric, usually made of cotton.

Prêt-a-porter—is a French term describing ready-to-wear collections. It is designed to be more widely available and attached to a lower price point, compared to haute couture garments from most design houses.

Puff Sleeve/Pouf Sleeve—a full sleeve of varying lengths, created by generous gathering around the armhole.

Pump—slip-in shoe with a medium to high heel, that can be used for day or night.

Purl Stitch—knitting stitch employed to create a ribbed effect.

Rayon—is a silky, lustrous material that is man made from natural fibers and has excellent drape and dyeability.

Saddle Stitch—small running stitches visible on the outside of a shoe, handbags, and other accessories.

Safari Style—safari-style garments adapted from bush jackets worn by hunters on African safaris, including such features as bellows pockets, belting, and epaulettes.

Sateen—lustrous cotton or rayon, this fabric has a smooth hand with a soft sheen.

Seersucker—term derived from the Persian "shirushaker," a kind of cloth, literally "milk and sugar." The woven crinkle is produced by alternating slack and tight yarns in the warp.

Shelf Bra—is a bra that is built into a garment and offers the support without being visible. It provides a smooth, seamless appearance.

Shrug—is a short jacket that is waist length or shorter. Some styles may look as if they only consist of a back and sleeves. A shrug is very similar to a bolero jacket.

Silhouette—is a shape of a garment from top to bottom; the key shapes a designer uses in his show indicate what silhouette people will be wearing. Popular silhouettes are A-line, H-line, Bell shaped, Empire line, etc.

Silk—an extremely soft, natural fabric made from the secretions of silkworms.

Sling-back—any shoe with an open back and strap around the heel.

Spaghetti Strap—a thin, tubular strap that attaches to the bodice, named for its likeness to a strand of spaghetti.

Stilettos—are either pumps or sling-backs with a high narrow heel. Usually used in the evening to dress up an outfit.

Straight Leg—a term used to describe pant legs that are cut in an equal width from the waist to the ankles.

Tankini—is a two-piece bathing suit with the upper portion resembling a tank top. Tankini provides the coverage of a maillot and the freedom of a bikini.

Trapeze Top—tank-top style with a fuller bottom sweep.

Trench—a waterproof overcoat styled along military lines.

Tumbled Leather—soft leather fabric with a slightly pebbled grain.

Tweed—a coarse wool or synthetic fabric used chiefly for casual suits and coats with subdued and interesting color effects.

Vamp—is the upper part of a shoe or boot covering the instep.

Vintage—describes a trend in fashion that references designs and other details from past eras, the 1920s to the 1970s.

Wide Leg—pants or jeans that are cut extra full through the legs with a wider leg opening.

APPENDIX B
Fashion Quotations

Enlarge the quotations and print out to use as decoration in the programming area or in the teen area to promote fashion programs.

"Personal style comes from within. It's when the woman, her individuality and spirit come through. She uses clothes to express who she is and how she feels."

—Donna Karan

✧ ✧ ✧

"For me, personal style is about that crazy composition. It's what I love about fashion. A bit boyish, but a bit sensual. A bit street, but a bit couture. It's all about deliberate nonchalance."

—Vera Wang

✧ ✧ ✧

"Personal style is being yourself."

—Diane Von Furstenberg

❖ ❖ ❖

"Personal style is having the confidence to be who you are, not necessarily flamboyant or eccentric. It can be as simple as turning up a cuff or the contradiction of a weathered motorcycle jacket slung over an elegant evening dress. It's taking a risk, and having fun with fashion, but always being true to yourself."

—Ralph Lauren

❖ ❖ ❖

"I think personal style starts from within because it's a philosophy and attitude. If you're honest and true to yourself, you will have the best sense of personal style. If you try and be someone else, it will never work because it's always very transparent when somebody is trying to mimic someone else. Less is always more with personal style. Just know yourself, know what works for you and be naturally confident in expressing that."

—Stella McCartney

"A girl should be two things: classy and fabulous."

—Coco Chanel

✧ ✧ ✧

"I wish I had invented blue jeans. They have expression, modesty, sex appeal, simplicity — all I hope for in my clothes."

—Yves Saint Laurent

✧ ✧ ✧

"The best thing is to look natural, but it takes makeup to look natural."

—Calvin Klein

✧ ✧ ✧

"When in doubt, wear red."

—Bill Blass

✧ ✧ ✧

"Fashion anticipates, and elegance is a state of mind … a mirror of the time in which we live, a translation of the future, and should never be static."

—Oleg Cassini

✧ ✧ ✧

"I've always thought of the T-shirt as the Alpha and Omega of the fashion alphabet."

—Giorgio Armani

APPENDIX C

Fashion Designers Trivia Quiz

Note: These are examples. You will need to add many more designers for this if it is going to last as long as 7 minutes. These are also suggested for use in the Fashion Designers Trivia Numbered Chairs game in Appendix X.

Label is DKNY, less expensive line for younger women, nickname "Queen of Seventh Avenue," well known for her "Essentials" line, seven easy pieces that could all be mixed and matched.
   Answer: Donna Karan

Trained as a figure skater, when she failed to make the U.S. Olympics team she entered the fashion industry. She was inducted into the U.S. Figure Skating Hall of Fame in 2009, being honored for her contribution to the sport as a costume designer. She opened her own design salon that features her trademark bridal gowns in 1990.
   Answer: Vera Wang

In 1970, with a $30,000 investment, she began designing women's clothes. When she was about to marry the second time, she decided to have a career. She wanted to be someone on her own, not just a plain little girl who got married beyond her desserts. She is best known for her wrap dress and signature prints.
   Answer: Diane Von Furstenberg

As a student at MTA (Marsha Stern Talmudical Academy), he sold neckties to his fellow students. He also went to DeWitt Clinton High School, where, when asked what he wanted to do in life, he stated that he wanted to be a millionaire. He did not attend fashion school but worked for Brooks Brothers as a salesman. Later, he opened a necktie store where he sold ties of his own design, under the label "Polo." He is best known for his Polo clothing brand.
   Answer: Ralph Lauren

This designer has a famous musician for a father. She became interested in designing clothes at thirteen when she made her first jacket. For her graduation collection the models included friends and supermodels Naomi Campbell, Yasmin Le Bon, and Kate Moss. She designed for Paris fashion house Chloe.
   Answer: Stella McCartney

She was a pioneering French fashion designer, whose modernist-thought, menswear-inspired fashions and pursuit of expensive simplicity made her an important figure in 20th-century fashion. Her extraordinary influence on fashion was such that she was the only person in the couturier field to be named on "Time 100: The Most Important People of the Century."
    Answer: Coco Chanel

At the age of twenty, this French designer found himself the head designer for the House of Dior. He was the first designer to use ethnic models in his runway shows and to reference cultures other than European in his work.
    Answer: Yves Saint Laurent

He is an American fashion designer. He was one of several design leaders raised in the Jewish immigrant community in the Bronx, New York. He became the toast of the New York elite fashion scene before he had his first mainstream success with the launch of his first jeans line.
    Answer: Calvin Klein

This designer was born in Indiana. The margins of his school books were filled with sketches from Hollywood-inspired fashions. At the age of fifteen, he began to sew and sell evening gowns for $25 each to a New York manufacturer. His designs were known for being wearable when other designers were designing works of art. He designed clothing that any woman could wear day or night.
    Answer: Bill Blass

A French-born American designer rose to prominence when he was chosen by Jacqueline Kennedy to design her state wardrobe. He was the exclusive wardrobe designer for his American film actress wife, Gene Tierney, in the 1940s and 1950s.
    Answer: Oleg Cassini

This designer is Italian and noted for his menswear. He is known for his clean, tailored lines. This designer was the first designer to ban models with a body mass index under 18. He was also the first to broadcast his collection live on the Internet.
    Answer: Giorgio Armani

I like things full of color and vibrant.
    Answer: Oscar de la Renta

APPENDIX D

Personal Style

Help find your personal style by completing the following.

1. Circle the words that best describe your personal style:

Funky	Polished
Classic	Girl
Fun	Upscale
Comfy	Crazy
Shiny	Flirty
Rock Star	Sophisticated
Posh	Mod
Sleek	Vintage

List your favorite:

2. Top 3 Designers

_____

_____

_____

3. Top 3 Fashion Trends

_____

_____

_____

4. Top 3 Accessories

_____

_____

_____

5. Top 3 Fashion Basics

_____

_____

_____

Look through magazines and clip out images that represent the things you listed above. Now you are ready to create an inspiration board.

APPENDIX E
Fashion Match Up

Cargo Style

Straight Leg

Pencil Skirt

Mini Skirt

Trench

Halter

Empire Waist

Cap Sleeve

Capri

APPENDIX F

PVC Pipe Clothes Hanger

Supplies:

- Four 36-inch lengths of 1-inch PVC pipe
- Four 12-inch lengths of 1-inch PVC pipe
- Two 1-inch, 4-way couplers
- Six 1-inch elbows
- PVC pipe glue

Equipment:

Hacksaw

If you don't have access to a hacksaw, the hardware store will cut the pipe for you. Many hardware stores are now selling short lengths of pipe.

Instructions:

- Dry fit all the pieces together first. Once the rack has been properly assembled, take it apart and reassemble, putting PVC pipe glue on the inside of the fittings (elbows and couplers) or the outside of the pipe. The glue should cover about ¾" of the fitting or pipe.
- Place two 12-inch pipes horizontally on each of the 4-way couplers.
- Place two 36-inch lengths of pipe in the vertical holes of the couplers.
- Place the 36-inch pipe coming up from the bottom into the down facing part of the elbow and the top of the pipe into opening that is facing inward.
- Once you have the hanger assembled, take it apart and apply the PVC glue using the applicator that comes with the glue. Let dry at least 20 minutes.

4-way inch coupler

1 inch elbow

APPENDIX G

Recipes for Spa Experience

Strawberry Hand and Foot Scrub

Strawberries contain a natural fruit acid which aids in exfoliation.

Ingredients:

- 8–10 strawberries
- 2 tablespoons apricot oil (you may substitute olive oil)
- 1 teaspoon coarse salt, such as kosher salt or sea salt

Mix together all ingredients into a paste, massage into hands and feet. Rinse and pat dry. The mixture is a bit messy, so protect floor and clothes.

Foaming Honey Foot Bath

Ingredients:

- 1 tablespoon honey
- 1 tablespoon liquid dish soap
- 1 teaspoon vanilla extract
- 2 tablespoons sweet almond oil (can be found in drug stores)

Mix all these ingredients together in a bowl and it's ready for your foot bath. Soak feet 10 to 15 minutes in warm water with the Foaming Honey Foot Bath.

For larger quantities use: ¼ cup honey, ¼ cup liquid soap, 1 tablespoon vanilla extract, and 1 cup sweet almond oil. Mix all ingredients together and store in a pretty bottle.

Rainbow Fruity Bath Salts

Ingredients:

- 3 quarts of Epsom salts or course sea salts
- 3 envelopes unflavored, unsweetened Kool-Aid powder, one each of three different colors
- 3–4 drops of scented essential oils which compliment the flavors of Kool-Aid, orange oil with orange, lavender oil with grape, and peppermint oil with strawberry, etc.)

Mix one envelope of Kool-Aid to 1 quart salts in three separate bowls. Add 3–4 drops of essential oils to each of the three bowls, with a scent that coordinates with the color. Let salt and Kool-Aid mixture sit briefly to absorb, approximately 15 minutes. Alternate the salt in colored layers in a glass or plastic container. To use, add ½ to 1 tablespoon per bath. Note: The Kool-Aid will NOT stain your skin or tub, but your white towels are another matter! Careful!

Avocado Face Mask for Dry and Sensitive Skin

Ingredients:

- 1 avocado
- 3–4 drops of almond oil

Peel and mash avocado and add almond oil until the mass is consistent. Apply to face while massaging it gently. Let it rest for 30 minutes and rinse off with warm water.

Moisturizing Avocado Facial Mask Recipe

Ingredients:

- 1 avocado
- 1 teaspoon of apple vinegar
- 1 egg white
- 3 teaspoons of olive oil

Peel and mash avocado and start adding the rest of the ingredients. Egg white should be beaten before you put it in. When the mask is done, apply to face and wash off after 20 minutes or so. This mask provides great moisture for skin, making it soft and elastic. http://www.skin-care-recipes-and-remedies.com/avocado-facial-mask-recipes.html

Yogurt Face Mask for All Skin Types

This simple (only two ingredients!) cooling mask is great for soothing a sunburned face. It's great for all skin types.

Prep Time: 2 hours

Total Time: 2 hours

Ingredients:

- 1 tablespoon natural yogurt, room temperature (not low fat or non-fat)
- 1 teaspoon runny honey (microwave for a few minutes to soften hardened honey)

Combine mixture, then apply to face. Let sit for 15 minutes. Wash face with steaming washcloth. Put washcloth in microwave to get it steaming, only a few seconds. For dry skin, use an extra teaspoon of honey. Oily skin? Add a few drops of fresh lime juice. www.about.com/beauty

Chocolate Facial Mask

This decadent mask is actually an excellent moisturizer, and it leaves your face baby soft. Recommended for normal skin.

Ingredients:

- ⅓ cup cocoa powder
- 3 tablespoon heavy cream
- 2 teaspoon cottage cheese
- ¼ cup honey
- 3 teaspoon oatmeal

Mix all ingredients together (a blender is ideal) and smooth onto face. Relax for ten minutes, wash off with warm water.

Sensitive Skin Cucumber Mask

This mask is perfect for sensitive skin. Chill in refrigerator before use to make it especially soothing.

Ingredients:

- 1 tablespoon brewer's yeast
- 1 tablespoon finely ground oatmeal
- 1 whole cucumber
- 2 tablespoons plain yogurt or sour cream
- 1 teaspoon honey

Mix together the yeast and oats in a small bowl and set aside. Peel the cucumber and place in small food processor and process until only liquid remains. Add the yogurt and honey and process further to mix. Add the brewer's yeast and oats to the cucumber/honey mixture and process to mix fully. Apply to clean face and neck skin and leave on for anywhere from 15 minutes to a half hour. Rinse well.

APPENDIX H

Test Your Knowledge about Semi-precious Gems

1. This gem is formed from a sticky resin that oozed from ancient pine trees. This gem usually has small insects, plant material, and other small objects trapped in it. Its colors range from dark brown to light, almost lemony.
   Answer: _____

2. This gem is formed from jadeite and nephrite, which are very similar in appearance. Jadeite is more intense in color and translucent, which brings a high price. The most valuable of this gem is the Imperial, which is found in Myanmar.
   Answer: _____

3. The top quality color for this gem is a deep grass green with a blush of blue. Because this gem contains many cracks, fissures, and inclusions, the majority are oiled. This means they are immersed in oil, which reduces the visibility of the imperfections and improves the clarity of the gem. The majority of this gem is found in Columbia and Brazil.
   Answer: _____

4. This gem is a member of the quartz group chalcedonies. It is one of the chatoyant gemstones which exhibits changeable, silky luster as light reflects on it. Because of the minerals in the stone, there are varying degrees of hardness, making it difficult to polish without undercutting.
   Answer: _____

5. This gem is an allotrope of carbon, in which the carbon atoms are arranged in variations of face-centered, cubic crystal structures. This gem is renowned as a material of superlative physical qualities. It has the highest hardness and thermal conductivity of any bulk material. The prepared gems are sold in exchanges called bourses, and there are only twenty in the world.
   Answer: _____

6. The purple variety of this quartz family is the most valued.
   Answer: _____

7. This gem is organic, and it takes seven to eight years to build a solid one. The most valuable are perfectly symmetrical, relatively large, and shimmering in luster. The principal area for these gems is found in the Persian Gulf.
   Answer: _____

111

8. For centuries the most valuable of this gem were found in Iran. Today, many of the specimens of this gem are mined in southwestern United States. The Persian gem does not have the black or brown veining commonly found in U.S. gems.
   Answer: _____

9. For centuries the world's main source of this gem has been the Mogok Valley in upper Myanmar. This gem's color varies from pink to blood red. The most valuable are pigeon blood red.
   Answer: _____

10. The red and pink variety of this gem was used in the jewelry of the Russian Czarinas of the eighteenth and nineteenth centuries and is often called "Imperial." One of the world's most important collections of this gem is found in the Green Vault in Dresden.
    Answer: _____

11. This gem is the non-red variety of the corundum; the red variety is the ruby. It is the second hardest natural mineral. Blue is the most popular color, but this gem can be almost any color.
    Answer: _____

Answers:

1. Amber
2. Jade
3. Emerald
4. Australian Tiger Eye
5. Diamond
6. Amethyst
7. Pearl
8. Turquoise
9. Ruby
10. Topaz
11. Sapphire

APPENDIX I

Jewelry Trivia Quiz

1. The American Arts and Crafts Movement started in the 1890s. Jewelry focused on color and the female form, mainly rendered through the use of enameling techniques. The motifs included orchids, irises, pansies, vines, swans, peacocks, dragonflies, and mythological creatures. One of the best-known artists was Rene Lalique, working in Paris. In Europe, the American Arts and Crafts Movement was known as _____.

2. Following World War I, the perceived decadence of the turn of the twentieth century led to simpler forms of jewelry. Jewelry was mass produced, making it accessible to more people. The philosophy was "no barriers between artist and craftsmen" and led to interesting and stylistically simplified forms. New materials, plastics and aluminum, were introduced to the public. This period is known as _____.

3. In 1831, an eighteen-year-old young woman became Queen and ruled until 1901. Like many teenagers she loved jewelry. She designed it, wore it, and gave it as gifts. She popularized charm bracelets and necklaces. This period of history is named for this queen. She was _____.

4. Her reign is broken into three periods. The second period is known as the _____ era (1849–1880) and corresponds with the death of the queen's husband, Prince Albert. The queen and her husband were very much in love. After his death the queen would only wear black. Most of the jewelry during this period was solemn and grave, known as mourning jewelry. The pieces featured heavy, dark stones. The more colorful designs featured shells, mosaics, and colorful gemstones.

5. The third period, 1880–1901, was known as the _____ period. The jewelry featured diamonds and colorful gemstones.

6. Silverworking was adopted by the Navajo when Mexican silversmiths traded their work for cattle. The Zuni admired the silverwork so much they began to trade livestock for lessons working in silver, and they then taught the Hopi. One of the favorite semi-precious gems to use in the silver setting is turquoise. In which region of the county is this style of jewelry known? _____

7. Necklaces are known by their length. A necklace that sits high on the neck and is 14 to 15 inches long is known as a _____.

8. A single strand necklace 22 to 23 inches long that rests at the top of the cleavage is a
   _____.

9. A necklace that sits at the breastbone and is 30 to 35 inches long is called what length?
   _____

10. Any necklace that is longer than 35 inches is called a _____.

11. A long necklace without a clasp that is draped multiple times around with the ends, roped over and looped or knotted, is a _____.

12. Any jewelry worn around the wrist is a _____.

13. In 2003 a yellow "Live Strong" bracelet was introduced by Nike and Lance Armstrong. These bracelets where made from colored silicone rubber. The silicone bracelets became a tool for awareness information and charity campaigns. These bracelets are known as
    _____.

14. In 1987, Chris Evert, famous athlete, was participating in her sporting event when her elegant, light, in-line diamond bracelet accidentally broke, and the event was interrupted to allow Chris to recover her precious diamonds. This type of bracelet sparked a new huge jewelry trend. This is the origin of the _____.

15. A bracelet with charms, decorative pendants, or trinkets that are significant to the wearer's life is a _____. Traditional charms dangle. A new trend is the Italian charms, which are soldered flat onto the surface of the link.

16. Bracelets worn in groups so that arm movements make a gracious sound are known as
    _____.

Answers:

1. Art Nouveau
2. Art Deco
3. Queen Victoria
4. Mid-Victorian
5. Late Victorian or aesthetic jewelry.
6. Southwest
7. Choker
8. Matinee necklace
9. Opera length
10. Rope
11. Lariat
12. Bracelet
13. Sports bracelets
14. Tennis bracelet
15. Charm bracelet
16. Bangles

APPENDIX J

Match the Type of Jewelry

Note: For this exercise you will need to go to the Internet and download photographs of each of the pieces of jewelry to be matched. You might ask your teen club to help with this, perhaps by finding examples and doing their own photography.

Match the type of jewelry to the picture of that piece of jewelry.

1. Early Victorian or Romantic	
2. Bangles	
3. Opera	
4. Mourning or Middle	
5. Victorian	
6. Bracelet	
7. Lariat	
8. Late Victorian or Romantic	
9. Rope	
10. Southwestern	
11. Art Nouveu	
12. Matinee	
13. Choker	
14. Sports	
15. Charm	
16. Art Deco	

From *Teens Have Style!: Fashion Programs for Young Adults at the Library* by Sharon Snow and Yvonne Reed. Santa Barbara, CA: Libraries Unlimited. Copyright © 2013.

APPENDIX K

Unscramble the Gems

Note: You will need to have pictures placed onto this page before you print it for your participants (http://www.bernardine.com/gemstones/gemstones.htm).

Each of the pictures is a gem, but the name next to it is incorrect. Put the correct gem with its name.

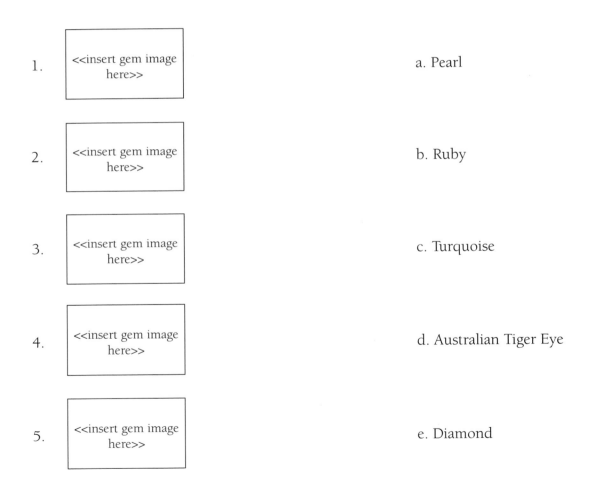

1. <<insert gem image here>>   a. Pearl

2. <<insert gem image here>>   b. Ruby

3. <<insert gem image here>>   c. Turquoise

4. <<insert gem image here>>   d. Australian Tiger Eye

5. <<insert gem image here>>   e. Diamond

6.   <<insert gem image here>>   f. Topaz

7.   <<insert gem image here>>   g. Emerald

8.   <<insert gem image here>>   h. Amethyst

9.   <<insert gem image here>>   i. Amber

10.   <<insert gem image here>>   j. Sapphire

11.   <<insert gem image here>>   k. Jade

APPENDIX L

Shoes throughout History Trivia Quiz

About the game:

The questions test teens about shoes and their history. These questions can be used in one of two ways: 1) Use them for a game of Number Chairs, and 2) Use them as an icebreaker for a shoe program with teens walking around the room, introducing themselves to other teens they don't know, and seeing if they can answer any of the questions. Find some shoe items, shoe key chains, shoe laces, other items, which can be found at Oriental Trading Company, for the teen who gets the most answers right in the shortest amount of time.

The questions are:

1. Which century was known for its high heels with lots of embellishments for women and extravagant embellishments and equally ostentatious shoes for men with a more modest heel? This century has a famous saying, "Let them eat cake."

   - 17th
   - 18th
   - 15th
   - 13th

Answer: 18th

During the 1700s, especially the 1740s to about 1790, shoes took on a life almost their own! Hair fashion during this time reached a peak of extravagance of style (think of Marie Antoinette), and shoes followed suit. De rigueur for the female were very high heels and brocaded or silk embroidered uppers, often complemented with a painted feather and almost always with a large, showy buckle. The males, not to be outdone, wore mostly black, medium-heeled, pointed shoes, decorated by large shiny gold or silver buckles. After the start of the French Revolution, excesses in shoe fashion rapidly declined, and more affordable styles with virtually no heel, manufactured from more practical and affordable leathers, became the fashion.

2. "Anything goes" was the motto of the 1970s. Disco fever was hot when this style of shoe reached its peak. What style of shoe was "hot"?

    •   Red high to tennis shoes
    •   Mary Janes
    •   Waffle stompers
    •   Platform shoes

Answer: Platform shoes

Remember "Saturday Night Fever" or any of Elton John's 1970s film clips? The chunkier and higher, the more sought after they were! Cork and solid wooden soles abounded. While we might like to believe they are a 20th-century creation, the reality is that the Ancient Greeks and Romans wore elevated shoes, and in 16th-century Venice, these shoes were worn by "ladies of the night." Japanese geishas also favored the style as a height-increasing accessory. Everything old is new again!

3. Another style that came from the 1950s and is still popular today was created by Louis Jordan. What are these "killer" heels called?

    •   Ice picks
    •   Stilettos
    •   Needles
    •   Winkle pickers

Answer: Stilettos

The iconic stiletto was a curved "vampish" shape with very high heels. They first became fashionable in the 1950s (among certain types of women). They were an alternative to light pumps and "court shoes," which were the epitome of conservatism.

4. Who was the shoe designer who constructed his first pair so his sister could have new ones for her First Communion? He designed shoes for Hollywood stars. After studying anatomy, he added steel inserts for arch support. He returned home to Italy and set up shop in Florence.

    •   Andre Perugia
    •   Bruno Magil
    •   Salvatore Feragamo
    •   Manolo Blahnik

Answer:

Perugia did indeed create shoes for Hollywood stars (e.g., Rita Hayworth and Gloria Swanson), but he was French, not Italian. Manolo Blahnik is from Switzerland, although his shop is in Italy. He also keeps well-heeled stars well heeled; Madonna and Bianca Jagger are devotees, and Carrie Bradshaw, one of the characters on "Sex and the City," owned miles of his stilettos. Bruno Magli is originally from Bologna, and his shoes are more widely distributed.

5. How did Doc Martens get their name?

- German physician
- Skinhead musician
- Marten Bulgaria
- A trucker

Answer: German physician

A German physician, Klaus Maerten, invented the air-cushioned soles of these shoes, supposedly after injuring his ankle skiing. When he later looked to license his product internationally, the British company that bought the patent rights anglicized the name. In the 1970s the shoes became the standard uniform of certain segments of the youth subculture. In 2003, declining sales forced the company to close the UK factory, and the shoes are now built in Asia.

6. The Lotus shoe style was worn in which country for almost one thousand years?

- Japan
- China
- Korea
- Thailand

Answer: China

Foot binding for females commenced in the Royal Palaces of China in the mid 10th century. Many myths make suggestions for what prompted this painful, disfiguring practice, but the generally accepted theory is that Prince Li Yu, the ruler of ten kingdoms in southern China, was enamored of a concubine called Precious Thing, who danced on her toes on a six foot high platform shaped like a lotus flower. To gain the Prince's favor, the other concubines began to walk on their toes and eventually foot binding was used to make the feet appear smaller and aid toe walking. The bound feet were clad in highly embroidered lotus shoes made of silk with a high heel. Originally foot binding was only practiced by the wealthy classes, but by the beginning of the 17th century, all classes had adopted the practice.

A law was passed in 1911 outlawing foot binding, but it still persisted in some areas until Mao Zedong came to power in 1949.

7. What is the earliest recorded date of shoe exports to England from the American colonies?

- 1640
- 1680
- 1650
- 1700

Answer: 1650

After observing the American Indian practice of producing comfortable moccasin-style shoes, the colonists started making their own. They were made from animal hides and proved to be so popular in England that the first pairs were exported in 1650. It was not until 1760, however, that the first mass production shoe factory was established in Massachusetts.

8. Which athletic footwear manufacturer created a new era in marketing and shoe fashion when it sponsored tennis player Ilie Nastases in the 1970s?

- Reebok
- Converse
- Adidas
- Nike

Answer: Nike

Nike (named for the Greek Goddess of Victory), is instantly recognizable for the "Swoosh" logo and "Just do it" slogan, commenced life in 1964 as Blue Ribbon Sports. The first footwear to carry the "Swoosh" logo was released in 1971, and by 1980 Nike had approximately fifty percent of market share. The waffle design sole was developed specifically for athletes, but now approximately half the general population, sporty or not, own a pair.

9. Espadrilles were originally created by Catalonian farmers. They called the shoes "alpargates." To what does the name "espadrille," which originated in France, refer?

- A shoe designer
- Espana
- Esparto grass
- A Riviera resort

Answer: Esparto grass: Esparto grass is a wiry, fibrous grass which was woven into rope for the soles of espadrilles. Many designers have adopted the espadrille style.

10. After coming home from a hunting trip with sopping wet feet, which man was inspired to create the "Maine Hunting Shoe" with a waterproof sole?

- Dick Cabela
- Alvah Curtis Roebuck
- Leon Leonwood Bean
- John Fry

Answer: Leon Leonwood Bean

L. L. Bean sold his boots through the mail, initially by contacting everyone with a valid Maine hunting license. The company prospered and now sells all sorts of clothing and outdoor supplies. Frye boots have been made since 1863 but are more suitable for riding than for slogging through marshes. Sears and Roebuck sold their share of boots, but Roebuck was a watchmaker, not a shoemaker. Cabela's sells boots, too, but started as a Nebraska outfit selling fly fishing supplies.

11. What is the name for the Japanese shoes that are thong sandals with a wood sole raised up on two wooden strips?

- Zori
- Geta
- Tabi
- Yukata

Answer: Geta

Geta are noisy shoes to wear; the onomatopoeic term for the sound is "karan-koron." It also takes some practice to balance properly on them. Zori are flat sandals without a separate heel. Tabi are the socks with a cleft between the great toe and the second toe to accommodate the thong of zori or geta. Yukata is a type of light, summer kimono.

APPENDIX M

Shhh Bingo

For this fashion Bingo game, the librarian will need to create several Bingo cards with scrambled numbers on them. Each vertical row on the card will contain scrambled numbers 1–5, and each card should have the numbers in a different order. A sample blank card has been provided as well as a sample of a finished card with the scrambled numbers.

The five letters across the top of the game, B-I-N-G-O, each represent a different area of fashion: B—Fashion words, I—Shoes, N—Hairstyles, G—Hats, O—Handbags. The librarian will need to create the cards used for drawing numbers in the game. Each card will have a different fashion term and number on it. Therefore, since B=Fashion words, there can be cards to pull that might say "B5 —Boot cut 5", "B3—Vintage 3", "B2—Trench 2", "B1—Halter 1", etc. A sample list of cards is provided here, but the librarian will need to create more to ensure that the teens can achieve Bingo. A list of helpful terms to use has been included.

To play the game, the leader will pull a slip of paper, announce the fashion terms and number, and teens will then fill in their box with a marker (a supply of buttons works well as markers in this game). The first person to get five in a row horizontally, vertically, or diagonally wins the game.

B I N G O

Fashion words	Shoes	Hairstyles	Hats	Handbags
		FREE		

B	**I**	**N**	**G**	**O**
Fashion words	Shoes	Hairstyles	Hats	Handbags
2	4	2	3	5
5	1	5	4	3
3	2	FREE	1	4
1	3	1	5	2
2	5	4	2	1

Sample list of cards to be drawn

B1 Boot-cut – 1	N4 Beehive – 4	B1 Pea coat – 1
B2 Cap Sleeve – 2	N5 Mohawk – 5	B2 Pencil Skirt – 2
B3 Cargo Style – 3	G1 Sunglasses – 1	B3 Baby Doll – 3
B4 Vintage – 4	G2 Belts – 2	B4 Drape – 4
B5 Paisley – 5	G3 Scarves – 3	B5 Cowl Neck – 5
I1 Ballet Flat – 1	G4 Necklaces – 4	I1 Stilettos – 1
I2 Flats – 2	G5 Tiara – 5	I2 Mary Jane – 1
I3 Sling-back – 3	O1 Anne Klein – 1	I3 Clog – 3
I4 Loafers – 4	O2 Chanel – 2	I4 Kitten Heel – 4
I5 Peep toes – 5	O3 Dickies – 3	I5 Espadrilles – 5
N1 Afro – 1	O4 Hollister Co – 4	N1 Chignon – 1
N2 Braid – 2	O5 Juicy Couture – 5	N2 Ringlets – 2

Fashion Bingo Terms

Fashion words:
1. Boot-cut
2. Bohemian
3. Cardigan Jacket
4. Chemise
5. Cowl Neck
6. Empire Waist
7. Paisley
8. Pencil Skirt
9. Peasant Top
10. Halter
11. Handkerchief Hen
12. Hip-Huggers
13. Inseam
14. Little Black Dress
15. Spaghetti Strap
16. Trench
17. Vintage
18. Wide Leg
19. Baby Doll
20. Tube Top
21. Bustier
22. Cap Sleeve
23. Cargo Style
24. Drape
25. Pea Coat

Shoes:
1. Ballet Flat
2. Clog
3. Mary Jane
4. Moccasin
5. Mules
6. Flats
7. Kitten Heel
8. Pump
9. Sling-back
10. Stilettos
11. Espadrilles
12. Loafers
13. Oxfords
14. Peep Toes
15. Spectator
16. T-Straps
17. Wedges

18. Wingtips
19. Sneakers
20. Doc Martins
21. Trainers
22. Sandals
23. Cowboy Boots
24. Ankle Boots
25. Uggs

Hairstyles:
1. Afro
2. Bob
3. Braid
4. Chignon
5. Cornrow
6. Crop
7. Dreadlocks
8. Extensions
9. Pony Tail
10. Beehive
11. Finger Wave
12. Gibson Girl
13. Ducktail
14. Pompadour
15. Buffet
16. Bowl
17. Mohawk
18. Buzz Cut
19. Flip
20. Page Boy
21. Shag
22. Emo
23. Bun
24. French Twist
25. Ringlets

Accessories:
1. Sunglasses
2. Purses
3. Hats
4. Belts
5. Scarves
6. Watches
7. Leg Warmers
8. Pins

9. Neckties
10. Broaches
11. Rings
12. Necklaces
13. Earrings
14. Bracelets
15. Toe Rings
16. Cuff Links
17. Wallet
18. Locket
19. Messenger Bag
20. Headbands
21. Bandanas
22. Hair Clips
23. Gloves
24. Charm Bracelet
25. Tiara

Designers or Popular Brands:
1. Anne Klein
2. Alexander McQueen
3. Calvin Klein
4. Christian Dior
5. Chanel
6. Giorgio Armani
7. Givenchy
8. Louis Vuitton
9. Michael Kors
10. Jimmy Chow
11. Victoria Beckman
12. Vera Wang
13. Abercrombie & Fitch
14. Dickies
15. Hollister Co
16. Juicy Couture
17. Rocawear
18. Nike
19. Urban Outfitter
20. Givenchy
21. Celine
22. Prada
23. Oscar de la Renta
24. Salvatore Ferragamo
25. Roxy

APPENDIX N

Famous Hats

This can be used as a trivia game which teens can play before or after a program, or it can be used as a numbered game activity.

<<Please place a picture of a beret here.>>	A. First worn in 1860 by the Brooklyn Excelsiors. By 1900 the "Brooklyn style" baseball cap had become popular.
<<Please place a picture of a cowboy hat here.>>	B. The Panama hat is a traditional brimmed hat of Ecuadorian origin, made from plaited leaves of the tequila straw plant. Early in the 20th century they were shipped from Panama. President Theodore Roosevelt wore one when visiting the Panama Canal construction.
<<Please place a picture of a Bicorn archaic (Napoleon's hat) here.>>	C. The top hat was created in 1793. It is usually associated with the upper class social society. President Abraham Lincoln wore and made popular a version of the top hat called the stovepipe hat.
<<Please place a bucket hat (as worn by Gilligan from Gilligan's Island on the 1965-1967 show) here.>>	D. A Russian ushanka, it can be tied up to the crown of the cap or tied at the chin to protect ears and jaws from the cold.
<<Please place the picture of a cloche hat here.>>	E. The cowboy hat is a fashionable and functional hat. The first cowboy hat was designed and constructed by J. B. Stetson in 1865.
<<Please place the picture of a stocking hat here.>>	F. A beret is a round hat that is usually made of soft wool.
<<Please place the picture of a beanie here.>>	G, Deerstalker, worn in rural areas for hunting. Most famous wearer of this kind of hat was the fictional character Sherlock Holmes.
<<Please place a picture of a fedora here.>>	H. Bicorn archaic is associated with 18th century military. Napoleon Bonaparte is famous for wearing this hat.
<<Please place the picture of a newsboy's hat here. >>	I. Gilligan, from the popular television from 1965–1967. Bucket hats are popular among men and women as a casual hat that offers sun protection.

<<Please place a picture of a sunbonnet here.>>	J. A beanie is a round, tight hat like a skullcap, formerly worn by schoolboys and young college students.
<<Please place the picture of a pokepie hat here.>>	K. The sombrero is a high-crowned hat of felt or straw with a very wide brim.
<<Please place the picture of a top hat here.>>	L. A stocking cap is a tightly fitting, cone-shaped, knitted cap.
<<Please place a picture of a sombrero here.>>	M. The fez is a hat that is in the shape of an abridged cone. Of Greek origins, this hat is not commonly worn today.
<<Please place a picture of a pillbox here.>>	N. Newsboys were popular around the turn of the 20th century. Often worn by young boys selling newspapers.
<<Please place the picture of a Panama hat here.>>	O. This hat was made famous in the movie "My Fair Lady." This style hat is often seen at the Kentucky Derby and at the Royal Ascot horse race in England.
<<Please place a picture of a fez here.>>	P. A fedora is a felt hat creased along the crown and pinched in the front of both sides. Worn by movie stars in the 1930s and 1950s. Typical headwear of film detectives and gangsters.
<<Please place the picture of a deerstalker hat here.>>>>	Q. A sunbonnet was worn by women to keep their skin lily-white. Made of some thin or light fabric projecting around the face. By the end of World War II, they were a thing of the past.
<<Please place a picture of a Russian ushanka here.>>	R. The cloche hat is fitted and bell-shaped, becoming popular from the 1920s until about 1933. Bonnie, in *Bonnie and Clyde*, wore a cloche hat.
<<Please place the picture of a baseball cap here.>>	S. Pokepie hat was part of the classic attire of American jazz and blues musicians. It has a short, indented top and sometimes a band.
<<Please place the picture of a hat that might be worn to Ascot or the Kentucky Derby here.>>	T. The pillbox hat is a small hat with upright sides and a flat crown made popular in the 1960s by Jacqueline Kennedy.

Hats, Hats, and More Hats Quiz Reference Scavenger Game

For this game, participants will need access to a computer and the Internet. It will test their searching skills. (Note: for answers 11 and 14, participants will need access to a printer to print the pictures they find.)

1. Dr. Seuss's *Cat in the Hat* has how many red stripes and how many white stripes on his hat?

   Answer: 3 red stripes and 2 white stripes for a total of 5 stripes

   Source: http://wiki.answers.com/Q/How_many_strips_were_there_on_cat_in_the_hat's_hat

2. When is it appropriate to wear a top hat?

   Answer: As of the early 21st century, a top hat is usually worn only with morning dress or white tie, in dressage, as servants' or doormen's livery, or as a fashion statement.

   Source: http://en.wikipedia.org/wiki/Top_hat

3. Who wears a tam?

   Answer: Tam O'Shanter (often abbreviated as TOS or Tam) is the 19th-century nickname for the traditional Scottish bonnet worn by men. It is named after Tam O'Shanter, the eponymous hero of the poem by Robert Burns.

   Source: http://en.wikipedia.org/wiki/Tam_o'_Shanter_(cap)

4. Every year Queen Elizabeth has a garden party, and women who are invited usually wear a hat. Find the name of one or two hat designers in London who create these hats.

   Answer: Rachel Trevor-Morgan

5. What did U.S. aviators in World War II call their head coverings?

   Answer: Aviator "trapper" cap

   Source: http://www.uswings.com/avcap.asp

6. Copy the first stanza of a poem about a hat. Be sure to give the author and the title.

   Possible Answer: Sandburg, Carl, Poem: "Hats"

   Source: http://www.americanpoems.com/poets/carlsandburg/12907

7. How many hats did Bartholomew Cubbins have?

   Answer: 500 hats

   Source: http://en.wikipedia.org/wiki/Bartholomew_Cubbins

8. What is the name of the book in which the monkeys stole the hats?

   Answer: *Caps for Sale* by Esphyr Slodkina

   Source: http://childrensbookalmanac.com/2011/01/caps-for-sale/

9. When you are graduating from high school, you will wear a hat called a _____.

   Answer: Mortarboard.

   Source: http://en.wikipedia.org/wiki/Square_academic_cap

10. For many years, female swimmers in public pools were asked to wear a bathing cap. Why?

    Answer: To protect filters from becoming clogged with loose hair.

    Source: http://en.wikipedia.org/wiki/Swim_cap

11. Find a picture of a bathing costume with a hat worn by women in the early 20th century.

    Answer: http://www.google.com/imgres?q=bathing+costume+of+1920s

12. What is the material used in creating a Panama hat?

    Answer: "Carludovica Palmata," often referred to as "Jipijapa," "Jipi," or "Paja Toquilla."

    Source: http://www.cowboyhatinfo.org/panama_hats.html

13. What hat would you wear if you were going on Safari?

    Answer: The pith helmet, a lightweight, cloth-covered helmet made of cork or pith.

    Source: http://en.wikipedia.org/wiki/Pith_helmet

14. Find a picture of a hat that would have been worn by a male Pilgrim in early America.

    Answer: A Pilgrim's hat, also known as the capotain, has a tall crown and a relatively narrow brim, with a slight cone shape. It is commonly associated with the Puritan dress of the late 1500s to mid-1600s. Before the Puritans adopted the hat, a Pilgrim hat was a bit taller and had a slightly wider brim. It was also known as the cockle hat.

    Source: http://www.wisegeek.com/what-is-a-pilgrim-hat.htm

15. Compare the hat a gaucho wears to a traditional cowboy hat in the United States

    Answer: A gaucho hat is a flat-brimmed hat. A cowboy hat is a wide-brimmed hat, which evolved from the Mexican sombrero.

    Source: http://www.depts.ttu.edu/museumttu/Cowboys'%20Manual-English.pdf and http://www .hitching-post.net/history2.php

APPENDIX P
Famous Hat People

Numbered Chairs

Put three chairs in the front of the room, each with a different point amount taped to it. Divide the group into three teams. Each team is given an envelope with slips of paper that are the answers to all of the questions you are going to ask (plus a few distracters). You ask a question and the team decides on the answer. One person from each team grabs the slip of paper with the right answer and races to sit in the chair that will bring them the highest point total. At the end, whoever has the most points wins.

On slips of paper write the following names of famous people who have worn hats:

- Indiana Jones
- Jack Sparrow
- Charlie Chaplin
- Napoleon Bonaparte
- Uncle Sam
- Blues Brothers
- Cat in the Hat
- Zorro
- Robin Hood
- Freddy Krueger
- Santa Claus
- Tin Man
- Cowboy Hat
- Deerstalker Cap
- Wide-brimmed Yellow Hat
- Coonskin Cap
- Tricorn Hat

- White Navy Cap
- Pillbox Hat
- Top Hat

The questions are:

- Who had a great beard and was an honest man? (Answer: Abraham Lincoln)
- As the wife of the 35th President of the United States, this First Lady made the pillbox hat popular. (Answer: Jackie Kennedy)
- Who is the burger-obsessed character from the Archie comics who wore a crown beanie? (Answer: Jughead)
- Which fictional character, played by Bob Denver, wore a white navy cap and left a ship shipwrecked on an uncharted island? (Answer: Gilligan)
- Which military and political leader of France wore a tricorn hat? (Answer: Napoleon Bonaparte)
- Which movie character, wearing a tricorn hat, said, "This is the day you will remember, as the day you almost caught Captain—"? (Answer: Jack Sparrow)
- Who wore a coonskin cap and was the king of the Wild Frontier, who died at the Alamo? (Answer: Davy Crockett)
- Who was the guardian of a monkey who had a knack for getting in trouble with a hat? (Answer: The man in the wide-brimmed yellow hat)
- Which fictional detective, created by Sir Arthur Conan Doyle, wore a deerstalker cap? (Answer: Sherlock Holmes)
- Who wore a cowboy hat and rode a horse named Silver and said, "Heigh ho, Silver, away"? (Answer: Lone Ranger)
- Who wore a tin hat and was a companion of Dorothy and the Scarecrow? (Answer: Tin Man)
- Who wears a red hat and works with elves? (Answer: Santa Claus)
- Wearing a brown fedora, this character stole dreams. (Answer: Freddy Krueger)
- He was a rich man who wore a feathered hat and stole from the rich and gave to the poor. (Answer: Robin Hood)
- Wearing a gaucho hat and a mask, this swordsman always left his mark. (Answer: Zorro)
- This mischievous cat wore a stripped top hat. (Answer: Cat in the Hat)
- A symbol of the United States, who wears a top hat. (Answer: Uncle Sam)
- Who are Dan Akroyd and John Belushi? (Answer: Blues Brothers)
- Who was a military and political leader of France? (Answer: Napoleon Bonaparte)
- A silent film legend, he wears a tramp costume. (Answer: Charlie Chaplin)
- An archaeologist/adventurist, he never leaves his hat behind. (Answer: Indiana Jones)

APPENDIX Q

Name that Hairstyle

For this exercise you will need to find pictures of persons wearing each of the hairstyles below and then place them in random order for participants to match. You may wish to add other hairstyles to these for a longer activity. (For pictures of hair from all times, check out *Redbook* magazine, September, 2011, page 65.)

1. Duck Tail	<<Insert Hairstyle Image Here>>
2. Pixie	<<Insert Hairstyle Image Here>>
3. Bowl	<<Insert Hairstyle Image Here>>
4. Punk	<<Insert Hairstyle Image Here>>
5. Afro	<<Insert Hairstyle Image Here>>
6. Farrah Fawcett	<<Insert Hairstyle Image Here>>
7. Dreadlocks	<<Insert Hairstyle Image Here>>
8. Flip	<<Insert Hairstyle Image Here>>
9. Shag	<<Insert Hairstyle Image Here>>
10. Beehive	<<Insert Hairstyle Image Here>>

APPENDIX R

Hair through History Trivia

For pictures of hairstyles for all times, check out *Redbook* magazine, September 2011, page 65.

1. Which fashion icon in the 16th century set the trend for white complexion and red tresses?

    a. Marie Antoinette
    b. Lady Gaga
    c. Queen Elizabeth I

2. Elaborate wigs, mile-high coiffures, and high, decorated curls were popular in which century?

    a. 15th
    b. 21st
    c. 18th

3. Characteristics of the Victorian hairstyles were

    a. Long flowing hair hung loosely down the back
    b. Brightly colored hair that was cut very short
    c. Emphasized natural beauty: hair was sleek, shiny, and healthy

4. The Roaring Twenties saw the emergence of

    a. Short, bobbed hair
    b. Women wearing little makeup
    c. The first pony tails

5. Which of the following were **not** characteristics of 1940s hairstyles?

    a. Feminine, romantic style
    b. Hair covered with headscarf, knotted at the front
    c. Use of many wigs by women

6. In the 1950s, which was the hairstyle for men that was **not** popular?

    a. Duck Tail
    b. Mohawk
    c. Pompadour

7. The most popular hair color in the 1960s was

   a. Black
   b. Red
   c. Blonde

8. Toward the end of the 1970s, the chief characteristic of hairstyle was

   a. Punk
   b. Spiked hair, dyed a vivid primary or fluorescent color
   c. Manes of free-falling curls

9. In the 1980s, the star that set the style was

   a. Farrah Fawcett
   b. Madonna
   c. Elizabeth Taylor

Answers:

1. c   Queen Elizabeth I
2. c   18th Century
3. a   Long flowing hair hung loosely down the back
4. a   Short, bobbed hair
5. b   Hair covered with headscarf. knotted at the front
6. a   Duck Tail
7. c   Blonde
8. a   Punk
9. a   Farrah Fawcett

APPENDIX S

Glossary of Guy Styles

Putting it all together

Casual dressing

Start with a pair of jeans. You have choices with many different cuts. Below is a boot cut which is gently flared to a slightly wide hem. For something different try a pair of khakis.

Note: You will need to find pictures of a boot cut pair of jeans and a pair of khaki pants for here.

Here you need to add images of a T-shirt with an image, a polo shirt, a plain T-shirt, and a short-sleeved shirt.

In cooler weather, wear a sweater or layer. Add a cardigan sweater over a short sleeved shirt. Instead of a T-shirt or polo, wear a turtleneck or mock turtleneck sweater. You will need to find images of sweaters or other jackets.

You will need something to cover your feet. Please add pictures below of sneakers, boots, and loafers.

To complete the look add some accessories. This doesn't need to be jewelry but it should include a belt, to keep the pants in place. Add sunglasses and a messenger bag or backpack. Please add pictures of these accessories below:

For those occasions when you need to present a more polished image, such as a special date, church, or a job interview, wear a flat-front pant, in black, gray or dark brown. Please place pictures of three pairs of pants below:

A dress shirt is usually long sleeved, either a plain color or a small stripe. Dress shirts below:

Top off the look with a jacket, blazer, or cardigan sweater. A leather jacket will give the look a more casual dressy look. If the weather is too warm for a jacket, top off the outfit with a vest. You will need a dress jacket, a blazer, a leather jacket, and a vest below.

A pair of loafers or dress shoes. You might just move pictures of loafers or dress shoes from above.

Remember to wear a belt. A thinner belt is dressier than a large, heavy one. The belt and shoes should match the color of the pants. Wear brown shoes with brown pants. Wear a lightweight dress sock not an athletic sock.

Cargo pants are not for the fashion conscious male. These pants are very utilitarian. They work on weekends. Be sure not to overload all the pockets because that will make you look bulky. The footwear options are boots or sneakers.

What size?
The inseam is the measurement taken from the bottom of the groin area to the floor. The rise is the measurement taken from the bottom of the groin area to the top of the waist.

Pants should hit the shoes and break once. The socks should not be peeking out of the pant leg when standing.

What style of pant leg should be worn? Straight legs always look good and flatter most heights and builds. Skinny guys can get away with a tapered pant leg. A flared leg only works on tall guys and only on jeans.

Baggy pants are rarely a good idea unless you have your own rap label.

Pants:

Bootcut describes the pant where the leg gently flares to a slightly wide hem. Originally designed so cowboys could pull their pants over Western boots, this cut is now a staple in contemporary design.

Chino is a durable, medium weight, twill fabric generally made of cotton or a cotton blend. The fabric is used for men's sportswear and work clothes and is generally found in khaki color.

Khaki describes both a brownish tan color as well as a fabric.

Cargo pants are similar to khakis but the difference is having side pockets sewn onto the outer thighs.

Shirts:

Dress shirts have a button-down collar.

Sport shirts come in long or short sleeves. It is the same as long sleeve dress shirt, but has a looser fit and the collar is not buttoned.

Polo shirts have short sleeves. They have a collar and three or four buttons on the top of the shirt. It is considered a little dressier than the other short sleeve casual shirts.

T-shirts are a staple for most men's wardrobes. The T-shirt is a non-collared shirt. It comes in many colors and materials. This shirt offers comfort, being light and flexible.

Chambray is a lightweight plain-weave fabric usually made of cotton, which is combined with an indigo yarn and a white yarn to achieve a denim-like effect.

Types of necklines:

V-neck shirts are a type of neckline that forms a V at the front of the neck.

Crew neck is a simple round finished opening in the top of a garment that fits close to the neck. Most commonly crew necks are found on T-shirts and sweaters.

Turtleneck is a high-rise collar found on sweaters and shirts.

Mock turtleneck is a collar that is lower and usually looser than a turtleneck and is not turned over.

Sweaters:

Cardigan is a sweater that is closed at the front using buttons or zippers.

Pullover is a sweater that must be pulled over the head when putting it on.

Sweatshirt is a loose, collarless pullover usually made of a heavy cotton jersey.

Hoodie is a sweatshirt with a hood.

Vest is a sleeveless garment, often having buttons down the front, usually worn over a shirt.

Coats and Jackets:

Bomber jacket is a short jacket, usually leather, tightly gathered at the waist and cuff by elasticized bands and typically has a zipper front.

<u>Motorcycle jacket</u> is a short, close-fitting jacket that extends to the hips. It will usually have a zipper and studs.

<u>Blazer</u> is a single-breasted coat closely related to a suit jacket.

Shoes:

<u>Loafers</u> are low, step-in shoes with no shoelaces or buckles, often made from leather or suede.

<u>Dress shoes or oxford shoes</u> are shoes that lace up. Dress shoes are leather shoes.

<u>Wingtip</u> shoes are shoes that feature a toe cap that comes to a point in the center and spreads out toward the sides of the shoe. The shape resembles a wing.

<u>Sneakers</u> are footwear of flexible materials, typically featuring a sole made of rubber. Sneakers were originally sporting apparel but today are worn more widely as casual footwear.

Resources for Librarians

ABC of Men's Fashion by Hardy Ames, Harry Abrams, 2007
   Quote from book "A man should look as if he has bought his clothes with intelligence, put them on with care, and then forgotten all about them."

APPENDIX T

Hygiene High Jinks

1. What causes athlete's foot?

   - Too much sweat or moisture between the toes
   - Wearing high heels that are too small
   - Playing too many sports video games
   - Running long distances without proper shoes

   Answer: Too much sweat or moisture between the toes

2. If you have bad breath, you have—?

   - Halitosis
   - Foot in Month disease
   - Meningitis
   - Homeostatic

   Answer: Halitosis, a word that comes from the Latin *halitus* (breath) and the Greek *osis*, meaning an abnormal condition.

3. To treat jock itch, use—?

   - Petroleum jelly
   - Flour
   - Baking soda
   - Corn starch

   Answer: Corn starch helps to absorb moisture from the groin area.

4. Deodorants are used because—?

   - They stop you from sweating.
   - They eliminate your sense of smell so you can't smell the body odor.
   - They cover up the smell of your sweat with a nice smell.
   - They release a chemical into the sweat glands which makes the sweat smell nice.

143

Answer: Deodorants simply cover up the bad smell of your sweat. They are different from antiperspirants, which actually stop you from sweating.

5. The toothbrush was invented by—?

- The Chinese in the 15th century
- The ancient Egyptian pharaoh in 2000 B.C.
- Ben Franklin in 1773
- Colgate

Answer: The bristle toothbrush was invented by the Chinese sometime during the 15th century.

6. You should visit the dentist—?

- When you start school
- Once a month
- Once every 6 months
- Every time you change your toothbrush

Answer: It is generally recommended that you visit the dentist once every six months for a checkup.

7. Which of the following is NOT a guy's hairstyle?

- Afro
- Mullet
- Washboard
- Bowl Cu

Answer: The washboard is not a guy's hairstyle. It is an instrument used years ago to wash clothes.

8. The best way to shave is—?

- Back and forth or up and down with the grain of the hair
- In a clockwise circular motion
- Make a W first and then get the rest
- In a counterclockwise, circular motion

Answer: It's best to direct the razor back and forth, or up and down, with the grain of the hair.

9. To get rid of ear wax, you should—?

- Dig around with the end of your pencil and see what comes out.
- Put the showerhead about an inch away from your ear and turn on the water full blast.

- Carefully clean it out using a cotton swab.
- Get your friend to spit on his finger and twirl it around the inside of the ear.

Answer: Ear wax can be removed by carefully cleaning the inside of the ear using a cotton swab. Be careful not to push the swab too far into the inner ear. You could damage it. However, some doctors don't recommend you use cotton at all.

10. When should you wash your hands?

- Wash your hands if you are going to eat
- Every time you use the bathroom
- Every time you go poo
- Only when you have time and aren't in a hurry

Answer: You should always wash your hands with soap and water after using the bathroom.

APPENDIX U

Looking and Smelling Good

True and False Quiz:

1. Take a shower once a week.   T   F

2. Keep your shoes on at all times, except when going to bed.   T   F

3. Don't wear dirty clothes.   T   F

4. Don't wear the same T-shirt, socks, or boxers more than once.   T   F

5. Shampoo when you take a shower, at least once a week.   T   F

6. Use a lotion to smooth out dry skin.   T   F

7. Don't bother combing your hair; the wind or rain will just mess it up.   T   F

8. Brush your teeth every other day.   T   F

9. If feet sweat during the day, don't wear socks.   T   F

10. Keep your fingernails and toenails clipped and clean.   T   F

11. Use lots of cologne because people need to smell you coming.   T   F

12. Wash your face every day with face cleanser.   T   F

13. Deodorant is used to prevent armpit odor.   T   F

14. Don't bother to hang up clothes after wearing; they will just get wrinkled the next time you wear them.   T   F

APPENDIX V

Tips for the Well-Groomed Guy

The tips below could be put on a bookmark.

- Shower every day with soap/body wash. It's important to stay clean.
- Shampoo and condition hair as needed. Most people have to wash their hair every day to prevent grease and odor. Remember to scrub your scalp and rinse all of the product out of your hair.
- Use a lotion to smooth out dry skin.
- Clean and clip fingernails. Toenails count, too.
- Use an antiperspirant to prevent underarm odor.
- Brush your teeth and floss them after every meal, or at least two times a day.
- Wash your face every day with face cleansers to prevent acne.
- Wear socks when you wear shoes. Feet sweat a lot during the day, so your shoes will smell pretty bad if you don't wear socks.
- Take off your shoes as soon as you get home so they can air out and dry out.
- Comb your hair. Keep it nice and neat.
- Wear undershirts to help keep your regular shirt smelling fresher.
- Don't wear dirty clothes, ever.
- You can sometimes wear the same jeans twice. But don't wear the same T-shirt, socks, or boxers more than once.
- Don't use too much cologne, especially inexpensive brands. They usually smell cheap. Wearing less is more considerate. Remember, there is no such thing as too little cologne, but there is such a thing as too much.
- If they are not dirty, hang up clothes after wearing them. They will look better the next time you put them on, and it will impress your parents.

From *Teens Have Style!: Fashion Programs for Young Adults at the Library* by Sharon Snow and Yvonne Reed. Santa Barbara, CA: Libraries Unlimited. Copyright © 2013.

APPENDIX W

Fashion Icons Numbered Chairs Pictures and Questions

1. She was a popular star in the 1940s and 1950s and was famous for her trousers. (Kathryn Hepburn)

    [Put a photo of Kathryn Hepburn here.]

2. This decade saw women wearing shorter skirts, minimized the bust, and a low waistline. Fashions showed off women's legs. (1920s)

3. The _____ was the rise of wholesomeness. The fashions showed off the back of the dress, especially evening gowns. Women could be seen in trousers fashioned after mens wear. Jackets and dresses had broad shoulders and were narrow at the hips. (1930s)

    [Put a photo of Marlene Dietrich here.]

4. She was one of the leading ladies and fashionistas of the 1930s. (Marlene Dietrich)

5. Fashions during this decade were more pratical and masculine in style. There was a carryover of padded shoulders and trousers from the decade before. (1940s)

6. In the_____ women used paint to simulate stocking seams when they weren't wearing stockings. (1940s)

7. The popular head coverings in the 1940s were _____. (scarves)

    [Put a photo of Vivien Leigh here]

8. A popular actress who became famous for a green dress was _____. (Vivien Leigh)

9. In what decade did brand names became important to young people? (2000s)

    [Put a photo of Bette Davis here.]

10. Another popular star known for her sense of fashion was _____. (Bette Davis)

11. By the end of the _____ there was a return to feminity, the waist was corseted, hips were padded, and skirts were billowing. (1940s)

148

From *Teens Have Style!: Fashion Programs for Young Adults at the Library* by Sharon Snow and Yvonne Reed. Santa Barbara, CA: Libraries Unlimited. Copyright © 2013.

[Put a photo of Elizabeth Taylor here.]

12. This actress was especially fond of jewelry. (Elizabeth Taylor)

13. The first part of the _____ was overtly femine. Two of the popular couture designers were Chanel and Dior. (1950s)

[Put a photo of Grace Kelly here.]

14. This actress became not only an American princess, but a real princess. (Grace Kelly)

[Put a photo of Marilyn Monroe here.]

15. This actress was married to a famous baseball player and a playright. (Marilyn Monroe, Joe DiMaggio, Arthur Miller)

16. Clothing designed for teens as first introduced in the late _____. These first styles were tight sweaters, pointed bras, circular skirts, and tight trousers. (1950s)

17. The favorite color for the Beatniks of the 1950s was_____. (black)

[Put a photo of Jackie Kennedy here.]

18. This icon was the 20th century First Lady who brought fashion and style to the White House. (Jackie Kennedy)

19. The miniskirt was invented by Mary Quant in the early _____. (1960s)

[Put a photo of Twiggy here.]

20. This young model was popular in the 1960s for her very thin figure. (Twiggy)

21. Individuality was expressed in _____with a rebellion against imposed ideas of femi-nie beauty. (1970)

22. The late 1970s was influnced by which type of music? (Punk)

23. In the 1970s hair was _____, pants had legs that were_____, skirts were_____ and shoes had _____. (long, flared or bell-bottomed, long, platforms)

[Put a photo of Madonna here.]

24. Wearing underwear as outerwear was made popular by _____. (Madonna)

[Put a photo of Princess Diana here.]

25. _____ was the young princess who became one of the fashion icons of the 1980s. (Princess Diana)

26. The fitness decade with legwarmers, leggings, leotards, and track suits was the _____. (1980s)

27. Body art (tattoos) and piercings became acceptable in the _____. (1990s)

[Put a photo of Lady Gaga here.]

28. In the 2010s, _____ has become one of the celebrities who is setting fashion trends. (Lady Gaga)

[Put a photo of Kate, Princess of Cambridge here.]

29. The newest royalty to watch for style is _____. (Kate, Princess of Cambridge)

[Put a photo of Michelle Obama here.]

30. A casual style of bright colors, belts, flats, off-the-shoulder dresses, and sandals is worn by another first lady, _____. (Michelle Obama)

31. The 2010s will be known for _____. (any answer the teens want to give about their fashions)

32. Individuality was expressed in customized clothes and the ethnic look in _____. (late 1960s and early 1970s)

APPENDIX X

Fashion Designers Trivia Numbered Chairs

The questions for this Numbered Chairs game were also used for another activity described in Appendix C.

Labeled DKNY, this designer for a less expensive line for younger women, is nicknamed "Queen of Seventh Avenue" and is well known for her "Essentials" line. This line includes seven easy pieces that could all be mixed and matched.
    Answer: Donna Karan

Trained as a figure skater, she failed to make the U.S. Olympics team and entered the fashion industry. She was inducted into the U.S. Figure Skating Hall of Fame in 2009, honored for her contribution to the sport as a costume designer. She opened her own design salon in 1990, and it features her trademark bridal gowns.
    Answer: Vera Wang

Armed with a $30,000 investment in 1970, she began designing women's clothes. When she was about to marry for the second time, she decided to have a career. She wanted to be someone on her own, not just a plain little girl who got married beyond her desserts. She is best known for her wrap dress and signature prints.
    Answer: Diane Von Furstenberg

Enrolled as a student at Marsha Stern Talmudical Academy (MTA), he sold neckties to his fellow students. He also went to DeWitt Clinton High School, where, when asked what he wanted to do in life, he stated that he wanted to be a millionaire. He did not attend fashion school but worked for Brooks Brothers as a salesman. Later, he opened a necktie store where he sold ties of his own design under the label "Polo." He is best known for his Polo clothing brand.
    Answer: Ralph Lauren

Born to a father who was a famous musician, this designer became interested in designing clothes at thirteen when she made her first jacket. Her graduation collection included, as models, her friends and supermodels Naomi Campbell, Yasmin Le Bon, and Kate Moss. She designed for the Paris fashion house Chloe.
    Answer: Stella McCartney

Influencing fashion from her pioneering days, this French designer incorporated modernist thought in creating menswear-inspired fashions. Her pursuit of expensive simplicity made her an important figure in 20th-century fashion. Her extraordinary influence on fashion was such that she was the only person in the couturier field to be named on "Time 100: The Most Important People of the Century."
    Answer: Coco Chanel

Finding himself the head designer for the House of Dior at the age of twenty, this French designer was the first to use ethnic models in his runway shows and the first to reference cultures other than European in his work.
    Answer: Yves Saint Laurent

An American fashion designer, he was one of several design leaders raised in the Jewish immigrant community in the Bronx, New York. He became the toast of the New York elite fashion scene even before he had his mainstream success with the launch of his first jeans line.
    Answer: Calvin Klein

Born in Indiana, the margins of his school books were filled with sketches from Hollywood-inspired fashions. At the age of fifteen, he began to sew and sell evening gowns for $25 each to a New York manufacturer. His designs were known for being wearable when other designers were designing works of art. He designed clothing that any woman could wear day or night.
    Answer: Bill Blass

A French-born American designer rose to prominence when he was chosen by Jacqueline Kennedy to design her state wardrobe. He was also the exclusive wardrobe designer for his American film actress wife, Gene Tierney, in the 1940s and 1950s.
    Answer: Oleg Cassini

Born in Italy and noted for his menswear with its clean, tailored lines, this designer was the first designer to ban models with a body mass index under 18. He was also the first to broadcast his collection live on the internet.
    Answer: Giorgio Armani

I like things full of color and vibrant.
    Answer: Oscar de la Renta

APPENDIX Y

Anime Guys with Black Hair

Note: Pictures for this exercise may be found in Coolmenshair.com. You will need to take care to put the picture of the character with Hiei Spike Hairstyle in box A, Long black bedhead in B, etc.

A	Long black "bedhead" (B) The most common hairstyle for anime guys with black hair is the simple "bedhead" look.
B	Goku hairstyle (D)
C	Itachi long hairstyle (G)
D	Zero (code gease) hairstyle (C)
E	Hiei Spike Hairstyle (A) Spikes are a common feature of anime guys. The spikes can point forward or stand straight out from the head, depending on the character's status as villain or hero.

F	Takshi Morinozuka hairstyle (E)
G	Forward spike hair (F)

APPENDIX Z

Anime Trivia

Here are some trivia questions to get you started. Construct trivia questions from series that are popular with teens who use your libraries. Get teens more involved by asking them to submit questions a couple of weeks prior to the program.

In Mobile Suit Gundam, what was the name of the EFSF base in South America?
(Answer: Jaburo)

Which idealized character did Utena (Revolutionary Gir Utena) aspire to become like?
(Answer: A fairy princess)

What is a sukumizu?
(Answer: school-issued swimsuit)

Who is generally considered "The Godfather of Manga"?
(Answer: Osamu Tezuka)

Which animation studio produces the Anime series Berserk?
(Answer: OLM [Oriental Light and Magic])

What sound frequently used in anime can be heard in Japan throughout summer?
(Answer: the sound of cicadas)

What series of Manga was banned in the Chinese city of Shenyang in 2005?
(Answer: Death Note)

What is the Japanese term given to a person that is overly obsessed with Anime?
(Answer: Otaku)

Which manga made by CLAMP was named after a plant?
(Answer: Clover "Sakura" is Japanese for cherry blossom)

In what CLAMP Anime is there a little Persocon named Chil?
(Answer: In "Chobits" by CLAMP, a boy named Motosuwa Hideki, who works at a bar, found a Persocon in the garbage. He brought it home and named it Chil.)

155

How many siblings does Shinji have?
(Answer: None before Shinji. From "Evangelion," before Shinji was born, his father said to his mother that if the baby was a boy, he'll be called Shinji, and if the baby was a girl, she would be called Rei.)

Which word was "invented" by Sakura Kinomot?
(Answer: Hoe. Notice how Sakura from "Cardcaptors Sakura" said "hoe" often even though it's not a word.)

Index